*Your second amendment rights are inherent in the Constitution of both the United States and the State of Oregon. One still needs to know and understand all the laws that regulate your gun ownership and Kevin Starrett is the most knowledgeable person I know regarding the law and your rights to bear arms. Kevin's book will provide you with all the information you need to be a law abiding gun owner.*

— Senator Alan Olsen

*Kevin Starrett is an entertaining encyclopedia of anything "gun" in Oregon. Not only does he know the law, he is also a formidable watchdog for 2nd Amendment rights. Any serious gun owner needs to hear what Kevin has to say.*

— Senator Kim Thatcher

*Kevin Starrett and Oregon Firearms Federation labor mightily to keep Oregon gun owners informed on legislation affecting the right to keep and bear arms. It's in the interest of all who care about that right to support OFF's vital mission, both financially, and by acting as force multipliers to help counter the media-amplified reach of the citizen disarmament lobby.*

— David Codrea, *The War on Guns*

# Oregon's Gun Laws

A guide for gun owners in the Beaver State

Kevin Starrett

Creative Crisis Management Publishing
Canby, Oregon

Creative Crisis Publishing
PO Box 556
Canby OR 97013


Cover photo: Kevin Starrett
Design: Anita Jones, Another Jones Graphics


ISBN: 978-0-9774939-0-6

Attention instructors, clubs, organizations, and interested parties,
contact us for quantity discounts.

Updates to this book, if required, will be available free on the website of
the Oregon Firearms Federation, where you can also get up to the minute
information on your gun rights in Oregon.  www.oregonfirearms.org

Printed and bound in the United States.

# DEDICATION

This book is dedicated to Val Hoyle, who helped ram through the Oregon Democrats' ugliest and most cynical attack on law abiding gun owners.

You proved that even if you take a quarter million dollar pay off from a crackpot, New York megalomanic, you can still lose an election to a crackpot, Oregon megalomaniac.

# ACKNOWLEDGMENTS

Any project can be improved. Certainly that was the case with this book.

I want to thank the people who took time to read various drafts and not only point out typos and grammatical errors, but highlight parts that needed clarification and provide suggestions for improvements.

To Sally Klein, Mike Butler and my sons; Sam and Jack Starrett, thank you for your input.

I took all their suggestions. Any errors left in this book are entirely their fault.

# TABLE OF CONTENTS

# INTRODUCTION

This book is a re-write of an earlier version entitled "Understanding Oregon's Gun Laws". While there are many similarities, this book was started from scratch and contains no cut and paste's from earlier books, but a lot of it will seem familiar to anyone who has read the previous efforts.

In 2015, after many years with only minor changes in the law, Oregon took a hard left turn and with the help of millions of dollars of out-of-state money, the anti-gunners in the Oregon legislature were able to ram through SB 941, the worst piece of anti-gun legislation in Oregon history. SB 941 is discussed in Section 4.

There were several other changes that took place in the law that made me decide to start over rather than just make updates.

This book is a somewhat more in-depth version of a class on Oregon's gun laws that I have been doing for several years. I learned a lot from the many people who have taken this class and my hope was to make this book as streamlined as possible so readers could quickly find the answers to the questions they are most likely to have about owning and carrying guns in Oregon.

In the many years I have worked for Oregon Firearms Federation I have had the opportunity to watch the legislative process in action. From 1998, when OFF was founded, until 2015, virtually no serious anti-gun legislation passed, although an awful lot was introduced. For that I can only give the credit to the thousands of OFF supporters who took time to write and call legislators and show up to voice their positions at hearings and town halls. Given that we were almost always outnumbered in Salem, I simply cannot imagine how much worse things would be in Oregon had those folks not been there.

Oregon's gun laws are the result of many people with different points of view, and different self interests adding and combining ideas with the hope of gaining some kind of personal benefit. Usually these people don't talk to each other. In many cases the laws simply make no sense at all.

For example, for many years, Oregon law allowed a person with a felony conviction to petition the courts to have his rights restored to buy a gun. That's "buy" a gun. If he was successful, he could still not own the gun. When this was pointed out to members of the legislature it took months for them to even understand that this could not possibly be the intent of whomever wrote the law. Oregon Firearms Federation labored to get this fixed. And it was; for a very short time.

After a correcting bill was passed (without a single "no" vote even from the most anti-gun legislators) the bill's sponsor, (also a militant anti-gunner) believed he had somehow been duped by us and now even people in prison would be allowed to have guns.

The absurdity of this position requires no explanation, but that same legislator immediately started working to reverse the bill he had sponsored and carried on the Senate floor.

It took a while but he was able to eventually reverse many of the corrections that had been made. Your tax dollars at work.

In 2015 the legislature was trying to fix a long standing mistake in the statutes that prohibited retired police (who do not require concealed handgun licenses to carry concealed) from carrying guns in public buildings, where licenses holders are allowed.

It had long been known this was a problem, but they just never got around to fixing it until 2015. The vehicle for this fix was House Bill 2357.

It should have been simple. All that was needed was to add the words "honorably retired law enforcement officer" to several places in the statute that protected concealed handgun license holders. But nothing is simple in politics. At the demand of one particularly shrill anti-gun zealot, language was added to make sure that retired cops who were criminals did not get these protections. Of course there were already plenty of laws that made sure of that. As a result the bill was mangled. Let me give you a quote from Section 4 of the final bill.

> (b) A person may not use the affirmative defense described in subsection (3)(e) of this section if the person has been convicted of an offense that would make the person ineligible to obtain a concealed handgun license under ORS 166.291 and 166.292.

You really don't need to read the bill, that section will do. "A person may not use the affirmative defense described in subsection (3)(e)..."Ok, let's look at subsection (3) (e). Here is what it says in its entirety:

> (e) An honorably retired law enforcement officer.

That's the whole section. Do you see an "affirmative defense" described anywhere in that section? Me either. Ok mistakes happen, but this mistake was noticed before the bill was signed into law and was brought to the attention of the legislature. They knew it made no sense. Of course, it was never fixed. We can do that next year.

That same year a bill was requested that would have added Municipal and Justice Courts to the list of places that are off limits to concealed handgun license holders. Judges, DAs, and the usual army of anti-rights activists paraded before the House and Senate Judiciary Committees demanding this protection.

When we pointed out that they already had that protection, that any judge in either of those courts could ban guns anytime he wanted to, that many already had, that this was settled law as a result of a lawsuit that OFF paid for, and that this whole waste of time could be avoided if judges in those courts would simply pay attention to current law, the Chairman of the House Judiciary Committee responded by saying "Well...it can't hurt."

Oregon Senator Mark Haas introduced a bill to outlaw the sale of privately owned, legal, ivory. There was an exception for ivory that comprised less than 20% of a gun or knife "by volume." When asked on the Senate floor how you measure the "volume" of a gun, he responded "By volume."

That's how we roll in Oregon. Whoever invented the comment about never wanting to watch sausage or the law be made clearly had watched both.

Anyone who has any faith in human nature can pretty much count on losing it if they spend any time watching what goes on under almost any capitol dome. A regular observer of the proceedings in the Oregon legislature, for example, would have the opportunity to hear complete and utter nonsense in hearings and floor speeches by legislators demanding an end to the sale of guns on Craig's List. (Craig's List has never allowed the sale of firearms.) He may have heard anti-gun activists, who regularly complain that Oregon concealed license holders lack training, testify against a bill that would allow more training facilities to be built. If he was really lucky, he may have heard this riveting quote from Senate President Peter Courtney:

> "When I was a little boy my mother apparently would stand in the window of a kitchen in Falls Church Virginia and she watched her middle son with his little animal graveyard. He didn't understand it, under a chestnut tree. He buried a little frog, he buried a little bird, he didn't understand what was going on.. and that individual was named Peter. I eat meat, I eat chicken, I eat fish."

No, I have no idea what he was talking about either. These people can be loons, but someone has to watch them.

This book accurately reflects the laws that were in effect when it went to press. If the laws change for better or worse, free updates will be available on the website of the Oregon Firearms Federation.

While every effort has been made to ensure the accuracy of the contents, laws do change. It would be wise if you own guns in Oregon, or plan to, to pay attention to current events. Your rights are never safe as long as there are anti-gun billionaires ready to buy legislators.

Freedom isn't free. You only get to make a difference if you show up. To everyone who has, I thank you. To everyone who feels inclined to show up in the future; welcome aboard.

# SECTION 1
## THE "PRE-EMPTION STATUTE"

In order to have a good understanding of Oregon's gun laws, the best place to start is with Oregon's "pre-emption" statute, ORS.166.170:

State preemption:

(1) Except as expressly authorized by state statute, the authority to regulate in any matter whatsoever the sale, acquisition, transfer, ownership, possession, storage, transportation or use of firearms or any element relating to firearms and components thereof, including ammunition, is vested solely in the Legislative Assembly.

(2) Except as expressly authorized by state statute, no county, city or other municipal corporation or district may enact civil or criminal ordinances, including but not limited to zoning ordinances, to regulate, restrict or prohibit the sale, acquisition, transfer, ownership, possession, storage, transportation or use of firearms or any element relating to firearms and components thereof, including ammunition. Ordinances that are contrary to this subsection are void. [1995 s.s. c.1 §1]

In plain English what it means is that, with limited exception, only the legislature, not cities, counties, or any other municipal entity may regulate firearms. The entire purpose of this statute was to prevent a patchwork of laws as you moved though the state which could place gun owners in jeopardy by unwittingly violating some obscure regulation while traveling. Anti-gun activists have been trying to repeal this law for decades.

What are the limited exceptions to the pre-emption statute? ORS 166.172 allows cities to regulate discharge of firearms and ORS 166.173 allows cities and counties to regulate possession of loaded firearms in public places.

Let's be clear. Localities may not regulate *open carry*; they may regulate *loaded carry in public places*. Here would be a good place to define what a "public place" is.

1

ORS 161.015 defines "public place."

"Public place" means a place to which the general public has access and includes, but is not limited to, hallways, lobbies and other parts of apartment houses and hotels not constituting rooms or apartments designed for actual residence, and highways, streets, schools, places of amusement, parks, playgrounds and premises used in connection with public passenger transportation.

So as you can see, a "public place" is not necessarily "public property," it is any place the public would normally be expected to be allowed. So localities may regulate loaded carry in places like grocery stores. No current statute specifically regulates loaded carry on private property, but theoretically one could.

Multnomah County Courts have held that your front porch can be treated as a "public place" because the public "has access" to it. They have also ruled that your car must be treated like a public place for the purposes of enforcing gun laws. The Court's position on cars was that a car is not actually a "place" at all, but a "container" in a public place. This ruling is problematic for many reasons, not the least of which is that some people treat vehicles as domiciles. In at least one case we know of, a person charged with unlawful possession of a firearm in his car was acquitted  because he actually slept in the vehicle. Furthermore, Oregon law specifically allows unlicensed, concealed possession of handguns in "recreational vehicles". (ORS 166.250)

While the pre-emption statute specifically allows localities to regulate loaded carry, it's very important to note that these regulations *do not* apply to persons with Oregon concealed handgun licenses. (CHLs).

The pre-emption statute is important, not only for what it does, but for how often it is violated by government actors.

The Oregon University System, like many other state agencies, had a long standing "administrative rule" banning anyone from having firearms on their property.  A student at Western Oregon University was actually arrested there when it was discovered he was in possession of a handgun. Although charges were quickly dropped when the Oregon Firearms Federation intervened, the student was still suspended and subjected to a kangaroo court style inquisition. The Oregon Firearms Educational Foundation sued the University System and the courts found that, in fact, the University System had no authority to make a rule as sweeping as theirs because it violated pre-emption. While another ruling, in a case also funded by OFEF, stated that schools *may regulate* their employees' behavior, they *could not* have a blanket ban on all firearms in the possession of concealed handgun licensees. Of course, they have come back and attempted to reintroduce the ban under other names, but it continues to be our position that they cannot enforce a blanket ban on firearms possessed by CHL holders.

As noted, the preemption statute is violated regularly by government agencies including police departments, county commissions, and even county fairs, so it's important for gun owners to know their rights. It is not uncommon for signs to be posted in government buildings saying "No Firearms." Sometimes they even include a statute number. Often the statute has nothing to do with firearms possession in public buildings.

This statute has been in the crosshairs of anti-gunners since it was enacted. There have been many attempts to weaken or overturn it and we expect them to continue.

*"This is a ghost gun. This right here has ability with a 30-caliber clip to disperse with 30 bullets within half a second. Thirty-magazine clip in half a second."*

— California State Senator Kevin de Leon

# SECTION 2
## WHO MAY OWN GUNS IN OREGON

Persons prohibited from owning firearms in Oregon are described in ORS 166.250. They include:

A minor, who was found to be within the jurisdiction of the juvenile court for having committed an act which, if committed by an adult, would constitute a felony or a misdemeanor involving violence, as defined in ORS 166.470; and was discharged from the jurisdiction of the juvenile court within four years prior to being charged under this section.

A person who has been convicted of a felony.*

A person who was committed to the Oregon Health Authority under ORS 426.130.

A person with mental illness and subject to an order under ORS 426.130 that the person be prohibited from purchasing or possessing a firearm as a result of that mental illness.

A person subject to an order under ORS 426.133.

ORS 426.133 deals with mandatory outpatient mental health treatment and allows the courts to prohibit firearms possession by people in such programs.

ORS 166.255 prohibits the possession of firearms and ammunition by a person who is the subject of a court order that "restrains the person from stalking, intimidating, molesting or menacing an intimate partner, a child of an intimate partner or a child of the person; and was issued or continued after a hearing for which the person had actual notice and during the course of which the person had an opportunity to be heard and includes a finding that the person represents a credible threat to the physical safety of an intimate partner, a child of an intimate partner or a child of the person."

Furthermore this same statute bans firearms and ammunition from people who have "qualifying misdemeanors". "Qualifying misdemeanors" are domestic violence misdemeanors. In 1996 the "Lautenberg Amendment" was adopted into Federal law and created a lifetime prohibition on firearms and ammunition for anyone with a domestic violence misdemeanor. This incredibly broad and abusive law has ensnared countless people who were involved in what were often extremely trivial matters.

In many cases, issues that were not violent in any way became legal confrontations as a result of overzealous law enforcement and prosecutors. People have been encouraged to plead guilty to these misdemeanors with the assurance that this was the easiest and least expensive way to make the problem go away. Usually those people had no idea they would be losing their firearms rights for *life*. Lautenberg was retroactive. This meant that if you had been convicted of a "domestic violence" misdemeanor 30 years before the law took effect, you lost your gun rights.

As of 2007, ORS 135.385 requires that persons accused of domestic violence be informed that they will lose gun rights if they plead guilty or "no contest". Prior to this, countless Oregonians pled guilty to end their legal nightmares without knowing what they were giving up.

In order to lawfully possess firearms in Oregon you must be 18 years old; however a minor may possess a firearm, other than a handgun, if it was transferred to him by a parent or guardian. A minor may possess a firearm, including a handgun, *temporarily* for hunting, target practice or any other lawful purpose.

Federal law allows a minor to posses a handgun, temporarily, with the written approval of a parent or guardian under limited circumstances. These include:

in the course of employment,

in the course of ranching or farming or

for hunting, target practice or "course of instruction in the safe and lawful use of a handgun."

A minor may also be in possession of a handgun if he is using it in defense against an intruder in his home or a place where he is an invited guest.

In respect to hunting, target practice or firearms classes, a minor may transport a handgun unloaded, in a locked container directly to the location where those events are taking place. (18 U.S. Code § 922)

---

* There is one section of Oregon law that has caused tremendous confusion even for legal professionals. This is our "felon in possession of a firearm" statute. ORS 166.270 outlaws the possession of firearms by convicted felons. Section (4) of the statute states that the statute does not apply to a person who has had only one felony that was not a homicide or a weapons violation, if 15 years have passed since the person has been discharged from imprisonment, probation or parole. Many people read this to mean that a felon who meets

that definition can own firearms. It does not. It means he cannot be charged under that statute with the crime of "felon in possession" but he may still not own guns.

*"Mandating Government paperwork to register before we can exercise our most fundamental rights in any other context, sounds absurd. So I am honestly baffled that we are even debating this today."*

— Oregon House Representative Shemia Fagan February 20th, 2015 on the House floor discussing a bill on voter registration. Shortly after this Fagan voted for mandatory government paperwork to buy or sell a firearm.

# SECTION 3
## WHAT YOU MAY OWN

In Oregon we have no restrictions on the type or number of firearms you may own or carry.

All Federal regulations apply of course, so you must have the proper tax stamp and required approval for any item restricted by the National Firearms Act of 1934. These would include machine guns, short barrel rifles and shotguns, suppressors, and any firearms classified as "Any Other Weapon" under the act.

Oregon has no restrictions on magazines or feeding devices. Oregon has no capacity limits on ammunition. Oregon has no restriction on the manufacture of firearms from so called "80%" receivers. Naturally, Federal laws still apply so those must be obeyed when dealing with firearms of this type.

Oregon's only restriction on ammo is in ORS 166.350 and deals with restrictions on "armor piercing ammunition." Under this statute, it is unlawful to make, sell, buy, or possess:

> "handgun ammunition the bullet or projectile of which is coated with Teflon or any chemical compound with properties similar to Teflon and which is intended to penetrate soft body armor."

Never mind that bullets coated with Teflon were never "intended" to penetrate soft body armor. These bullets were originally created by three men, one of whom was a police sergeant. They found that the very hard bullets they had created to allow police ammo to penetrate hard targets like car doors, caused excessive wear on gun barrels. The Teflon coating was intended to reduce that wear. In 1982, NBC ran a misleading special on TV claiming these bullets were "cop killers" and falsely arguing that the Teflon coating would allow the bullets to defeat soft body armor. Anti-gun politicians and organizations parroted the lies and several states, including Oregon, restricted them. These bullets were never sold to civilians and never killed a single police officer.

Note: this only applies to handgun ammo. Also note that it also only applies if the person who possesses the ammo intends to use it in the commission of a felony, or if the person is actually committing a felony and that person or an accomplice is armed with a firearm. The entire statute follows.

**166.350 Unlawful possession of armor piercing ammunition.** (1) A person commits the crime of unlawful possession of armor piercing ammunition if the person:

(a) Makes, sells, buys or possesses any handgun ammunition the bullet or projectile of which is coated with Teflon or any chemical compound with properties similar to Teflon and which is intended to penetrate soft body armor, such person having the intent that the ammunition be used in the commission of a felony; or (b) Carries any ammunition described in paragraph (a) of this subsection while committing any felony during which the person or any accomplice of the person is armed with a firearm.

(2) As used in this section, "handgun ammunition" means ammunition principally for use in pistols or revolvers notwithstanding that the ammunition can be used in some rifles.

(3) Unlawful possession of armor piercing ammunition is a Class A misdemeanor. [1985 c.755 §2; 1987 c.158 §29]

We expect efforts to be made to restrict lead ammo in Oregon, but as of this writing no such statute has passed.

Concealed handgun license holders should be aware that while their permit allows them to carry and conceal as many firearms as they choose, it does *not* allow them to conceal other weapons. Under ORS 166.240 it is unlawful to carry "concealed upon the person":

"any knife having a blade that projects or swings into position by force of a spring or by centrifugal force, any dirk, dagger, ice pick, slungshot, metal knuckles, or any similar instrument by the use of which injury could be inflicted upon the person or property of any other person."

Note, these items are not banned under Oregon law, but they may not be carried concealed and a concealed handgun license does not exempt a license holder from this prohibition. Peace officers, however, are exempt. Violations are Class B misdemeanors.

# SECTION 4
## BUYING GUNS IN OREGON

As a result of the passage of Senate Bill 941 by Oregon Democrats in 2015, almost all private transfers of firearms are now unlawful. If you want to sell or transfer a firearm you must now have the transfer conducted by a Federally licensed dealer. He may charge whatever he chooses, if he is willing to conduct the transfer at all.*

A background check through the Oregon State Police is required with an additional fee. If the buyer is delayed, the transfer may be terminated there and then by the seller or, the dealer may keep the gun until the check is completed. He must then treat the firearm as though it was part of his own inventory.

If the buyer (or "transferee") is ultimately denied, the dealer must conduct a background check on the original owner before he can return it. The OSP background check system is notoriously inaccurate and people are frequently delayed or denied with no justification. If the original owner is denied when trying to get his property back, there is no provision in the law for the disposal of the firearm.

When a background check is conducted in Oregon, there are three possible outcomes: An approval, a denial, or a "pend" or delay. Both Federal law and Oregon State law allow a person who has been delayed to take possession of the firearm after 3 business days "have elapsed." The exact wording of the Oregon and Federal laws are somewhat different, but Federal law controls. The Feds' definition of 3 days "elapsing" means that if you initiate a background check on Monday, then Tuesday, Wednesday and Thursday must "elapse" and you can lawfully take possession of the gun on Friday. A "business day" to the Feds is any day State Offices are open.

Please note: this is law as of the time this book went to press. The anti-gun extremists in the Oregon Legislature have attempted to eliminate this small safeguard and force buyers to wait as long as the OSP wants to take. Please check recent changes in the law to determine if the "three day" safeguard is still in effect.

In reality very few dealers are willing to complete transfers without police approval. Many mistakenly believe they would face liability if they do. In fact, Federal law specifically protects gun dealers in this case. So while dealers *may* transfer on delayed transactions, they rarely do.

The background check is supposed to be "instant" but in fact can be indefinite. We know of people who have waited over 2 years for a background check to be completed. Incorrect results are common. We have seen people who have been approved for a transfer in one store and delayed in another store on the same day. There are instances of people being approved within minutes while still being delayed for transfers they attempted months before. The Oregon State Police ID Unit has a terrible and well deserved reputation for ignoring or stonewalling buyers who are attempting get their mistaken delays and denials corrected. Typically the only way to get a response from them on a request for a correction is to have a pro-gun legislator contact them. In those cases, the errors are usually corrected within hours. If you live in district with Democrat representatives, you are usually out of luck.

If you are delayed or denied for a firearms purchase, you should receive from the gun dealer a phone number for the State Police "ID" unit's "challenge line." In theory you should be able to call that number to find out what is causing your delay or denial. In reality, this is usually an exercise in frustration. You will *always* get a voice mail and there is no guarantee you will be called back. If you are, it will likely be when you are not home. If possible, always leave a cell phone number. The ID unit has no dedicated personnel returning calls of people seeking to correct their delay or denial. It is their policy to call gun buyers back when they have time and free personnel. Given the number of checks that need to be run now that you must have a check to give a gun to your best friend, call backs are erratic at best, as you can imagine.

There are exceptions for the mandatory background check/dealer transfer for some family members. They are:

A transferor's spouse or domestic partner;
A transferor's parent or stepparent;
A transferor's child or stepchild;
A transferor's sibling;
A transferor's grandparent;
A transferor's grandchild;
A transferor's aunt or uncle;
A transferor's first cousin;
A transferor's niece or nephew; or

The spouse or domestic partner of the persons specified above. Or,

The transfer of a firearm that occurs because of the death of the firearm owner, provided that:

The transfer is conducted or facilitated by a personal representative, as defined in ORS 111.005, or a trustee of a trust created in a will; and

The transferee is related to the deceased firearm owner in a manner specified above.

Note in Oregon, "domestic partner" does <u>not</u> mean a person of the opposite sex with whom you share an intimate relationship and with whom you live. Heterosexual couples cannot be "domestic partners." Only people of the same sex can be "domestic partners." So if you are living with a person of the opposite sex, you may not give or loan her a firearm no matter how long you have been together. Note also that the exceptions do not include "in-laws." If you want to transfer a firearm to your father-in-law, you must do it through a gun dealer or give it to your spouse who then gives it to his or her father. Under this idiotic system, guns can be transferred to persons not on the list of exceptions by creating a daisy chain of transfers from spouses to in-laws to cousin's cousin's stepchildren. It is little wonder the law was opposed by most Oregon Counties and many sheriffs have said they simply will not enforce it.

There are a few other exceptions to the mandatory background check, at least in theory. For example, you may allow another person to use a firearm you own if you are target shooting with them. You <u>may not</u> lend someone a firearm if they are going target shooting without you. You may also lend them a firearm for a safety class, but only if you are there with them. You may also lend them a firearm:

"For the purpose of hunting, trapping or target shooting, during the time in which the transferee is engaged in activities related to hunting, trapping or target shooting."

We believe that this means you can lend a person a firearm at the time of hunting, trapping or target shooting. While it is unclear, it is almost certainly a crime to lend someone a rifle on Thursday if he is going hunting on Friday.

You may transfer a firearm to a person who is in the business of repairing firearms or making or repairing firearms accessories.

There are a few other things you need to know about the effects of SB 941 from 2015.

The bill allows you to lend or "transfer" a firearm without a background check:

"for the purpose of preventing imminent death or serious physical injury, and the provision lasts only as long as is necessary to prevent the death or serious physical injury."

This language is so ambiguous that very few people would be willing to risk providing a firearm to another person. How do you prove someone is in "imminent" danger? How do you prove when that danger has passed? Who is in violation if the firearm is not returned? These and many other questions were presented to the Democrats who forced this bill through. All the questions were brushed aside or ignored completely.

The bill now makes it impossible for a person covered by the "Address Confidentiality Program" to buy a gun unless they get it from a close relative. People whose addresses are suppressed under this program do not have ID with a real physical address on it. (Their addresses are suppressed because of threats to their lives.) Because of that they are forbidden from buying guns from dealers. They cannot get guns from private parties anymore either. If they have no family members willing to provide firearms and they cannot prove the threat is "imminent," they are simply out of luck.

SB 941 outlaws the storage or safeguarding of a firearm for a friend or neighbor.

SB 941 outlaws the purchase of handguns by persons between the ages of 18 and 21. Prior to this law being enacted, an 18-year-old could purchase a handgun as long as it was from a private party. Since private parties can no longer transfer firearms without a dealer conducting the transfer, those sales are now illegal as well. Now the only option is to get a handgun from a family member.

SB 941 virtually eliminates any reasonable way for firearms to be part of an estate sale.

* One exception is for firearms transferred by private parties at gun shows where sellers can contact the State Police directly for a background check. Have your credit card ready.

# SECTION 5
## CARRYING GUNS IN OREGON

Oregon is an "open carry" state. This means that you do not need a license to carry a firearm as long as the firearm is not concealed. There are some restrictions however. First, we need to point out that there are different rules for carrying firearms for people who have concealed handgun licenses (CHLs) and people who don't. In most cases, it is unlawful for a person who does not have a CHL to carry a firearm concealed. There are exceptions:

(a) Members of any club or organization, for the purpose of practicing shooting at targets upon the established target ranges, whether public or private, while such members are using any of the firearms referred to in ORS 166.250 upon such target ranges, or while going to and from such ranges.

(b) Licensed hunters or fishermen while engaged in hunting or fishing, or while going to or returning from a hunting or fishing expedition.

Be careful with those definitions. The courts have taken a very narrow view of what it means to be "going to or returning from a hunting or fishing expedition." Basically, you'd better not be making any stops along the way.

Almost none of the restrictions that can be applied to non-licenseholders apply to those with licenses.

Concealed handgun license holders are not allowed to carry firearms in court facilities, federal buildings, or private property where the owner prohibits guns.* *(Remember, "public places" can still be private property as noted in section 1 on the pre-emption statute).* Those are the only restrictions in Oregon for license holders.

Oregon CHLs are honored in some other states, but states do sometimes change their rules. If you are traveling to another state, be sure to check their rules before you carry a gun there with an Oregon CHL. There are excellent sources online that keep track of which states honor which permits. At this time Oregon recognizes the permits of no other states.

Non-licenseholders are also barred from the places where CHL holders are prohibited of course, but they are also not allowed to carry in "public buildings."

According to ORS 166.360:

"Public building" means a hospital, a capitol building, a public or private school, as defined in ORS 339.315, a college or university, a city hall or the residence of any state official elected by the state at large, and the grounds adjacent to each such building. The term also includes that portion of any other building occupied by an agency of the state or a municipal corporation, as defined in ORS 297.405, other than a court facility.

Furthermore, non CHL holders are required to obey local regulations regarding loaded carry in public places as discussed in section 1.

As noted there, localities *may* regulate loaded carry. Some cities have such bans. Since these change, it's always wise to check local regulations. While in most places a person without a license can carry openly, there are places like Portland, Salem, and McMinnville where non CHL holders must carry unloaded. In Portland, you may not even be in possession of a loaded magazine, although we think it's doubtful that would withstand a legal challenge.

The enforceability of these laws is complex. It is totally lawful, even in places with loaded carry restrictions, to carry a firearm openly with an unloaded magazine inserted in the firearm. There is usually no way to determine if a magazine is loaded without inspecting it. Police have no authority to inspect a firearm in the absence of suspicion of a crime, and while they might do it, they can't do it legally.

There is one exception to this. A peace officer may inspect a firearm to determine if it is loaded in a public building. (ORS 166.380) This law makes no sense at all. When it was amended in 2015, this was pointed out, but that made no difference to the legislators who amended it.

First of all, if you do not have a CHL you are not allowed in a public building with a firearm at all. Second, if you do have a CHL, your gun may be loaded. So what's the point? In 2015 the law was changed so a person with a CHL could provide his license rather than providing the gun for inspection. However, police have no authority to demand to see your license under these circumstances and there is no penalty for refusing to provide your license.

One more thing to note about carrying firearms. If a person does not have a CHL and he wants to transport a gun but he is either walking or taking public transit, (or riding his double decker bike if he is in Portland,) the only legal way to do so is to carry the firearm openly. The gun may not be in a container, locked or otherwise. It may not be carried in a backpack or briefcase. It may not even be transported in its original box.

There are several rules that apply to carrying firearms in vehicles. Oregon has no statutes regulating the carrying of long guns in vehicles except for snowmobiles and ATVs. (See more on this below.) A gun owner may transport a rifle or shotgun any way he likes. It may be transported concealed or openly and no CHL is required. Oregon state law also makes no distinction between loaded and unloaded firearms for the purposes of transport in vehicles that are not snowmobiles or ATVs.

Of course, local restrictions on loaded carry still apply, so if you are not a CHL holder, and you are in one of those locations, your long gun may not lawfully be loaded.

Handguns may be transported in vehicles in two ways. (Once again, these restrictions do not apply to CHL holders who can carry any way they like.)

First, they may be carried openly. (Again, Oregon law makes no distinction between loaded and unloaded handguns for purposes of transport in vehicles, but local regulations on loaded carry still apply.)

Second, they can be transported concealed if they are "not readily accessible." For many years that term had no definition. Now it has a confusing one. Here is our best shot at decoding it.

If your vehicle has a trunk (or as the statute says, "a storage location that is outside the passenger compartment") the handgun must be there. If you are driving a conventional sedan, this is fairly straight forward. However, things become a lot less clear if you are driving something like a pickup truck. Is the bed of a pickup a "storage location?" What if it has a cap? Is a toolbox in the bed of a pickup truck a "storage location?" The statute does not address this.

If the vehicle does not have a "storage location" outside the passenger compartment, (for example, a minivan) the handgun may be transported:

> "In a closed and locked glove compartment, center console or other container; and the key is not inserted into the lock, if the glove compartment, center console or other container unlocks with a key."

Once again, the state makes no distinction between "loaded" and "unloaded" for the purposes of regulating the transport of handguns in vehicles that are not snowmobiles or ATVs but local restrictions on loaded carry apply to non-CHL holders.

The rules for transporting handguns on motorcycles, snowmobiles or ATVs require that for non-CHL holders who are not carrying openly:

> If the vehicle is a motorcycle, an all-terrain vehicle or a snowmobile, a handgun is not readily accessible within the meaning of this section if:
>
> (A) The handgun is in a locked container within or affixed to the vehicle; or
>
> (B) The handgun is equipped with a trigger lock or other locking mechanism that prevents the discharge of the firearm.

There are further regulations for non-CHL holders who are carrying guns on snowmobiles and ATVs.

While CHL holders are free to carry firearms on ATVs and snowmobiles any way they like, if you do not have a CHL, you may not carry openly or concealed, a loaded firearm while riding ATVs and snowmobiles . This restriction is not in ORS 166 where most gun laws are rather it is in our traffic regulations under ORS 821.240.

That brings us to what the term "loaded" means. Oregon law defines "unloaded" for when referring to carry on ATVs and snowmobiles and "loaded" when referring to carrying in public buildings and courts.

For purposes of carrying a firearm on an ATV or snowmobile "unloaded" means the following:

> (a) If the firearm is a revolver, that there is no live cartridge in the chamber that is aligned with the hammer of the revolver;
>
> (b) If the firearm is a muzzle-loading firearm, that the firearm is not capped or primed; or
>
> (c) If the firearm is other than a revolver or a muzzle-loading firearm, that there is no live cartridge in the chamber.

The second definition is in ORS 166.360 which deals with the regulations of firearms in courts and public buildings. There the term "loaded" means:

> (a) A breech-loading firearm in which there is an unexpended cartridge or shell in or attached to the firearm including but not limited to, in a chamber, magazine or clip which is attached to the firearm.
>
> (b) A muzzle-loading firearm which is capped or primed and has a powder charge and ball, shot or projectile in the barrel or cylinder.

The major difference in the definitions is that in public buildings a gun is loaded if there is a round in any way attached to the gun, while on snowmobiles and ATVs the gun is only "loaded" if, for semi-auto's there is actually a round in the chamber and for revolvers there is a round under the hammer. (Of course, if you are carrying a revolver with only the chamber under the hammer empty, the gun will still go bang if you pull the trigger. The lawyer who drafted this language appeared to be unaware of that and we felt no overwhelming need to explain it to him.)

Finally, a word about "brandishing." The first incarnations of this book can be traced back many years to an email question OFF received which prompted me to create the "FAQ" page on the Oregon Firearms Federation website which eventually became the first version of what you are reading now. The writer of the question had been told during the class she took to get her CHL, that when she got it, she lost her right to carry openly. That is, of course, nonsense. Oregon is an open carry state. A CHL is permission to carry concealed, not a mandate to carry concealed. If you are a license holder and someone sees your firearm, you are not "brandishing." You are not violating any law. In fact there is no "brandishing" statute in Oregon and I have never even seen the word appear in our laws. What we do have is a "menacing"statute and that is the law that often ensnares gun owners who have drawn firearms in self defense. In Oregon, menacing means the following:

> "A person commits the crime of menacing if by word or conduct the person intentionally attempts to place another person in fear of imminent serious physical injury."

That's pretty broad, and it has been over applied many times to people who simply displayed firearms when they have felt threatened, but to be clear, the fact that someone has seen a gun you are carrying is not a crime.

---

*Private property owners can trespass you off their property if they do not want you to be there with a firearm. Oregon has multiple trespass statutes, one being "trespass with a firearm." There are no laws in Oregon which require that private property have signs posted saying "No Guns." While it is unclear if and how a person could be prosecuted for trespass if he did not know the property owner prohibited firearms,we think it's possible.

*"What's the efficacy of banning these magazine clips? I will tell you these are ammunition, they're bullets, so the people who have those now, they're going to shoot them. And so if you ban them in the future, the number of these high-capacity magazines is going to decrease dramatically over time because the bullets will have been shot and there won't be any more available."*

— Rep. Diana DeGette (D-Colo.)

# SECTION 6
## STORAGE OF FIREARMS

At the time of this writing only Portland and Multnomah County have rules regulating the storage of firearms. Their regulations deal with minors gaining access to firearms.

They also have regulations requiring the reporting of stolen guns and the imposition of fines if the serial numbers of the guns cannot be provided to the police.

As we told you in Section 1, the Oregon pre-emption statute quite clearly limits the creation of regulations of this kind to the Legislative Assembly. We believe both of these regulations are unlawful. In one case a person who had two rifles stolen in Portland got a demand letter from the City to pay fines because he could not provide the serial numbers of the guns.

He contacted the Oregon Firearms Federation, whose lawyers then contacted the City of Portland and told them the fines would not be paid. Period. The City never said another word about it. As a result, the issue was never actually litigated, but we still believe the ordinances are unlawful.

As of the time this book was written, Oregon has no regulations on the storage of firearms. Once again, things change quickly and the anti-gunners have vowed to impose one-size-fits-all storage restrictions, so check for updates. Of course, responsible gun owners make decisions about storing firearms based on their personal circumstances. A person with no children or irresponsible visitors would obviously have different needs than a person who shared a home with people who should not have access to guns.

The Portland version of these ordinances are copied on the following pages. As we said, we don't believe these regulations are lawful.

### 14A.60.050 Endangering A Child By Allowing Access To A Firearm.

(Added by Ordinance No. 184274, effective December 31, 2010.)

A. A person commits the offense of endangering a child if a person fails to prevent access to a firearm by a minor when the person knew or reasonably should have known that a minor could gain access to the firearm under the following circumstances:

1. A person possesses or controls an operable firearm, whether loaded or unloaded, within premises under the person's custody or control and a minor gains access to the firearm without the permission of the person, a parent or guardian.

2. A person possesses or controls an operable firearm, whether loaded or unloaded, within premises under the person's custody or control and a minor gains access to the firearm without the permission of the person, a parent or guardian and the minor carries the firearm off the premises.

B. Violation of Subsection A.1. is punishable by incarceration for not more than 10 days and a fine of not more than $500.

C. Violation of Subsection A.2. is punishable by incarceration for not more than 20 days and a fine of not more than $750.

D. Violation of Subsection A.2. is punishable by incarceration for not more than 30 days and a fine of not more than $2,500 when the firearm is carried by the child off premises to any school, school-sponsored or school-related event.

E. Defenses: This section shall not apply if any one of the following circumstances exists:

1. The minor obtains the firearm as a result of an illegal entry into any premises by any person.

2. The firearm is kept in a locked container or in a location that a reasonable person would believe to be secure from entry by the minor.

3. The firearm is locked with a device that has rendered the firearm inoperable and is designed to prevent minors and unauthorized users from firing the firearm. The device may be installed on the firearm, be incorporated into the design of the firearm, or prevent access to the firearm.

### 14A.60.060 Failure to Report Theft.
(Added by Ordinance No. 184274, effective December 31, 2010.)

A. Any person who possesses, owns or controls a firearm in the City of Portland shall report the theft or misplacement of the firearm to the Chief of Police or designee, providing a description of the firearm including serial number, within

48 hours of knowing, or having reason to know, the firearm is stolen or cannot be located through reasonable effort.

B. A person who possesses, owns or controls a firearm in the City of Portland and fails to provide the serial number of the firearm when reporting the firearm is stolen or cannot be located is subject to a $200 administrative fee.

C. Violation of Subsection 14A.60.060 A. is punishable by a fine of $2,500

*"Do you know what a barrel shroud is?"*

— Tucker Carlson
MSNBC TV Host

*"I believe it's the shoulder thing that goes up."*

— Carolyn McCarthy
Former Congresswoman and anti-gun advocate.

# SECTION 7
## ALCOHOL AND FIREARMS

Oregon has no regulations concerning alcohol and firearms. There is no prohibition on carrying firearms in places that serve or sell alcohol. In fact there are no rules prohibiting consuming alcohol while carrying a firearm.

While there is no law stating it is unlawful to be legally drunk while in possession of a firearm, it certainly is possible for a sheriff to revoke a concealed handgun license from someone who is intoxicated and armed by using his power under ORS 166.293.

(2) Notwithstanding ORS 166.291 (1), and subject to review as provided in subsection (5) of this section, a sheriff may deny a concealed handgun license if the sheriff has reasonable grounds to believe that the applicant has been or is reasonably likely to be a danger to self or others, or to the community at large, as a result of the applicant's mental or psychological state or as demonstrated by the applicant's past pattern of behavior involving unlawful violence or threats of unlawful violence.

(3)(a) Any act or condition that would prevent the issuance of a concealed handgun license is cause for revoking a concealed handgun license.

*"Some of these bullets have an incendiary device on the tip of it which is a heat seeking device. So you don't shoot deer with a bullet that size, if you do you could cook it at the same time."*

— Former New York Assemblywoman Patricia Eddington

# SECTION 8
## REGISTRATION OF FIREARMS

When a firearm is purchased in Oregon a background check is conducted by the Oregon State Police (often very badly.)

They collect information on the buyer of the gun (and also the seller if the seller is a private party transferring through a gun dealer) plus the make, model, caliber, and serial number of the gun being sold or transferred. Legally they are allowed to keep this information for 5 years.

Although the OSP has stated empathically that they do not share this information, make no back-ups and destroy it after 10 days, researchers have demonstrated this to be false. The idea that a state agency has no system for backing up their databases is absurd and even though the State of Oregon has demonstrated that its agencies are not very good with computers, rest assured this information is being kept.

In this regard, those firearms are "registered." However, there is no system of "registration" for firearms acquired elsewhere. So if you, for example, move to Oregon from another state, there is no requirement to "register" your guns and no process for doing so. This is also true for firearms transferred within Oregon between family members. So if granddad gives you a firearm, there is no "registration" process. Note: Oregon law does not allow for a license to purchase, own or possess a firearm in your residence or place of business. Residences include recreational vehicles and vessels. "Place of business" means a business you actually own, not simply where you work. The only firearms licenses Oregon has are concealed handgun licenses which will be discussed in section 9.

*"We have Federal regulations and state laws that prohibit hunting ducks with more than 3 rounds. And yet it's legal to hunt humans with 15-round, 30-round, even 150-round magazines."*

— California Senator Diane Feinstein

# SECTION 9
## CONCEALED HAND GUN LICENSES

Concealed Handgun Licenses are regulated under ORS 166.291. CHLs are administered by the County Sheriff. The law specifies that the forms used to apply be in "substantially" the same format. To get a CHL you must be at least 21 years old.

You may not be a felon unless your record has been expunged or you have had your gun rights restored under ORS 166.274 or 166.293 or section 5, chapter 826, Oregon Laws 2009, or 18 U.S.C. 925 ( c ). For more info see section 13 "Rights Restoration".

You must not have had any misdemeanors within the last 4 years.

You must be a citizen of the United States or you must be a legal resident alien who has declared intention to become a citizen. If you are a legal resident alien, you must have lived in the county in which you are applying for six months. This six month requirement does not apply to US Citizens.

You must not have been found to be a person with mental illness or subject to an order under ORS 426.130 that you be prohibited from purchasing or possessing a firearm as a result of that mental illness.

You must not have been committed to the Oregon Health Authority under ORS 426.130.

You must not be subject to a stalking order or a restraining order.

You must not have received a dishonorable discharge from the military or be required to register as a sex offender in any state.

You must not have been convicted of a "offense involving controlled substances." This one is very broad but there is an exception. Prior to Oregon legalizing pot, a person who had been convicted of possession of a small amount of marijuana could still get a CHL if they had only been convicted once or only had one diversion, but not both. Now that pot is legal, the CHL law still says you can get a CHL if you have had one conviction of violating ORS 475.864(3)( c). That section used to make it a violation to have less than an ounce of pot. Now it makes it a violation to have less than an ounce of pot <u>if you are under 21.</u> Keep in mind, pot is still illegal under Federal law. While it is perfectly legal to have an Oregon CHL if you smoke or possess pot, *it is illegal under Federal law to smoke or possess pot and own a gun.*

The exceptions only cover marijuana-related offenses, not other controlled substances. So for example, if you were convicted of a DUI and were under the influence of a prescription drug at the time, that would be an "offense involving controlled substances" and even if it was only a single offense, you would not be eligible for a CHL.

You must be a resident of the county in which you are applying unless you are applying for a non-resident permit. Currently only people who live in adjoining states may apply for non resident permits. While Oregon is a "shall issue" state for residents (meaning that if you meet the qualifications, the sheriff must issue the permit) this is not true for non-residents. Sheriffs have complete discretion to issue or not to a non-resident. Some sheriffs do; some don't. Some have issued for a while and then stopped. Some only issue to residents of certain counties in certain states. Oregon has no provision for non-residents whose permits have expired and are seeking renewals if the sheriff that issued decides no longer to do so. At least one county (Linn) was renewing non resident licenses that had originally been issued in other counties at the time of this writing.

A person is considered a "resident" of the county in which he is applying if he:

(a) Has a current Oregon driver license issued to the person showing a residence address in the county;

(b) Is registered to vote in the county and has a voter notification card issued to the person under ORS 247.181 showing a residence address in the county;

(c) Has documentation showing that the person currently leases or owns real property in the county; or

(d) Has documentation showing that the person filed an Oregon tax return for the most recent tax year showing a residence address in the county.

You must "demonstrate competency with a handgun" by any of the following:

(A) Completion of any hunter education or hunter safety course approved by the State Department of Fish and Wildlife or a similar agency of another state if handgun safety was a component of the course;

(B) Completion of any National Rifle Association firearms safety or training course if handgun safety was a component of the course;

(C) Completion of any firearms safety or training course or class available to the general public offered by law enforcement, community college, or private or public institution or organization or firearms training school utilizing instructors certified by the National Rifle Association or a law enforcement agency if handgun safety was a component of the course;

(D) Completion of any law enforcement firearms safety or training course or class offered for security guards, investigators, reserve law enforcement officers or any other law enforcement officers if handgun safety was a component of the course;

(E) Presents evidence of equivalent experience with a handgun through participation in organized shooting competition or military service;

(F) Is licensed or has been licensed to carry a firearm in this state, unless the license has been revoked; or

(G) Completion of any firearms training or safety course or class conducted by a firearms instructor certified by a law enforcement agency or the National Rifle Association if handgun safety was a component of the course.

The most common of these are firearms classes taught by NRA-certified instructors. Note, those classes are not required to be actual NRA approved classes. They only have to have handgun safety as a component and be taught by NRA-certified instructors.

As noted in Section 7 a sheriff can deny (or revoke) a CHL:

"if the sheriff has reasonable grounds to believe that the applicant has been or is reasonably likely to be a danger to self or others, or to the community at large, as a result of the applicant's mental or psychological state or as demonstrated by the applicant's past pattern of behavior involving unlawful violence or threats of unlawful violence."

Sheriffs are law enforcement officers and are not necessarily competent to determine what an applicant's "mental or psychological" state is. This part of the statute has been used by some sheriffs to deny with no history of crimes or violence.

Sheriffs have 45 days to issue or deny a CHL; however, there is no penalty in the statute if they don't. A person who is denied or revoked can petition the Circuit Court in the County of their residence within 30 days of denial or revocation. The statutes have no provisions for a non resident who is denied or revoked.

At the time this book went to press, CHLs cost $65.00 and were valid for 4 years. Renewals cost $50.00.

If you move within your county, a replacement CHL with your new address will cost $15.00. This is also the fee for replacing a lost CHL. If you move to another Oregon county, most, but not all counties will charge $30.00 for a "transfer." Some counties insist on new fingerprints, some do not.

Oregon law requires that you notify the sheriff of a change of address if you have a CHL, however, in spite of what many sheriffs have said, there is no statutorily mandated time frame for this requirement.

Licenses are valid for 4 years. Under ORS 166.295:

> "a license is renewable by repeating the procedures set out in ORS 166.291 and 166.292, except for the requirement to submit fingerprints and provide character references."

However in at least one county (Clackamas), renewals can now be done completely online. Why other Sheriffs are not using this system is a mystery.

Members of the military may renew by mail.

# SECTION 10
## INTERACTION WITH LAW ENFORCEMENT

If you are lawfully in possession of a firearm when you interact with law enforcement you may wonder what your obligations are.

While this can happen anywhere, it is most likely to happen while you are driving.

One of the most common questions people have when getting concealed handgun licenses is "What are my responsibilities if I am stopped by the police?"

Despite what many instructors say, you have absolutely no obligation to volunteer to a police officer that you have a CHL or a firearm. In fact, you have no obligation to have any conversations with the police. Once you have applied for a CHL, your name is entered into the Law Enforcement Data System. As soon as a police officer has identified you, in a traffic stop for example, he already knows you have a CHL. If you are driving a car that is registered to you, he knows this before he has even spoken to you, if he has run your license plate.

If you are stopped for an alleged traffic infraction, you are required to provide your driver's license, car registration and proof of insurance. You are not required to provide a CHL.

Whether you should or not is another question. There are still plenty of police who mistakenly believe you must volunteer this info and produce a CHL on demand. In fact, there are many police who believe they can seize your firearm for the duration of the stop. Some even think they can unload it. Well, of course they can, but it's not legal. Many instructors also believe this and others think that volunteering that you have a CHL is a wise courtesy. In reality, there is no reason to believe you will be treated any better because you have offered this information. While some police may appreciate the gesture, others have treated it like a threat.

In the end the choice is really yours. Some states require that you immediately inform police that you are armed. Oregon does not. In fact, the Oregon Supreme Court has ruled in *State of Oregon vs Joseph Lucio Jimenez* (2015) that police may not even ask you if you have a firearm unless they have a specific reason to believe they might be in danger.

*"There are a lot of people that have been shot by an unloaded gun and whether it's loaded or not, it still presents a threat.*

— Sandy Sheedy
Sacramento City Council Woman

# SECTION 11
## "STAND YOUR GROUND"

"Stand your ground" laws have become quite controversial. In Oregon, unlike in many other places, you have no duty to retreat from an attacker, anywhere.

While this has long been the law, it was misunderstood for far too long even by our own Courts.

The issue was resolved (at least for now) in 2007 in State of Oregon vs Sandoval. Some background from the decision:

> "Defendant (Sandoval) shot and killed his ex-wife's domestic partner, Whitcraft. The two men had a history of combative and sometimes physically violent interactions. The shooting occurred on a road that both men frequently traveled. When the police arrived on the scene, defendant described the following sequence of events: Whitcraft had driven by on the road as defendant was about to turn onto it; after defendant turned onto the road behind Whitcraft, Whitcraft stopped his truck and backed it into defendant's truck; Whitcraft then turned and aimed a pistol at defendant; defendant grabbed a rifle that he was carrying in his own vehicle (both men kept guns in their vehicles), opened the door of his truck and fired a single shot at Whitcraft. Investigators determined that the shot had entered Whitcraft's skull behind his left ear, killing him instantly. Police later found Whitcraft's loaded and cocked pistol under Whitcraft's body."

At the trial, the jury was given a series of instructions that largely echoed Oregon's laws regarding the use of deadly force. But in addition they were told:

> "The danger justifying the use of deadly force must be absolute, imminent, and unavoidable, and a necessity of taking human life must be actual, present, urgent and absolutely or apparently absolutely necessary. There must be no reasonable opportunity to escape to avoid the affray and there must be no other means of avoiding or declining the combat."

This of course, was 100% wrong.

The decision goes on:

> "As we shall explain, that instruction apparently was based, not on the statutes discussed below, but on this court's 1982 opinion in State v. Charles, ...

> Indeed, the entire analytical flow of the Charles opinion is distinctly odd: The court did not examine the wording of either ORS 161.209 or 161.219 at all. Instead, the court set out the wording that the Oregon Criminal Law Commission had proposed to the legislature regarding the use of deadly force as part of the final draft of the proposed 1971 Criminal Code, which wording explicitly imposed a duty of retreat to avoid the necessity of using deadly force. Then, after noting that the 1971 legislature had rejected that wording, the court cited a view expressed in the Oregon Criminal Law Commission's Commentary to the 1971 Code to the effect that "the statute probably was not necessary" because of existing Oregon case law. 293 Or at 278 (discussing Commentary to Criminal Law Revision Commission Proposed Oregon Criminal Code, Final Draft and Report § 23, at 23-25 (Jul 1970)). Then, without discussing at all the fact that the Oregon legislature had adopted statutes on the subject, the court concluded, inexplicably, that "Oregon case law * * * controls the subject." 293 Or at 277. The court then went on to discuss its prior cases (and to conclude that they did not support the defendant's claim that Oregon does not recognize a "duty of retreat.")

> Although, from our present perspective, it seems surprising that this court would attempt to answer the question presented in Charles without resort to the controlling criminal statutes, that is precisely what the Charles court did. The court's analysis did not focus on or even consider the words of the statutes that we now recognize to be pivotal. Neither did the court conclude, as the state suggests, that the drafters of ORS 161.219 had decided to "continue" the "common-law rules" as explicated in the various self-defense cases that preceded the enactment of that statute. Charles, therefore, has nothing to contribute to our present effort, which is to discern what the legislature intended with respect to the "duty of retreat" question.

> We conclude, in short, that the legislature's intent is clear on the face of ORS 161.219: <u>The legislature did not intend</u>

<u>to require a person to retreat before using deadly force to defend against the imminent use of deadly physical force by another."</u>*

It is rather chilling to realize that a person's freedom can hang in the balance of courts who so greatly misinterpret the language of Oregon's use of force statutes. While not as simple as they could be, they certainly should have been understood by Oregon's Courts.

We'll look at those statutes in the next section.

*Emphasis added

*If you want to protect yourself get a double barrel shotgun have the shells, the 12 gauge shotgun, and I promise you, as I told my wife, we live in an area that's wooded and somewhat secluded, I said Jill if there's ever a problem, just walk out on the balcony here, walk out, put that double barrel shotgun and fire two blasts outside the house -- I promise you whoever is coming in is not going... You don't need an AR-15, it's harder to aim, it's harder to use and in fact you don't need 30 rounds to protect yourself.*
*Buy a shotgun! Buy a shotgun!"*

— Joe Biden
Vice President of the United States

# SECTION 12
## USE OF FORCE AND DEADLY FORCE

The use of force in Oregon is governed by ORS 161.

As you have seen from the Sandoval case, the fact that the law says something quite specific does not mean you are protected simply because you followed it. That is where the danger is in the use of force.

It would be impossible and unwise to try to say "here is when you can use force." So instead, I've posted the most relevant statutes on the use of force. You should read them. Really.

Oregon recognizes two kinds of force: "physical force" and "deadly physical force".

The difference is pretty obvious. Holding someone, shoving him to the ground or kneeling on him while you wait for the police to arrive is "physical force." Anything you do that can or will kill him is "deadly physical force."

Basically Oregon allows you to use force against another person equivalent to the force they are using or threatening to use against you.

If someone pushes you, you can push them back. Shooting them would be frowned upon.

Oregon law does allow for deadly physical force in two circumstances where it is not necessarily being used against you:

If a person is committing a burglary in a "dwelling" or if a person is committing or attempting to commit an "arson or a felony by force and violence" in a "premises."

In this context a "dwelling" means a building which regularly or intermittently is occupied by a person lodging therein at night, whether or not a person is actually present. (ORS 164.205) A "premise" is a building but does not have to be a "dwelling."

So what is a "burglary?"

"A person commits the crime of burglary in the second degree if the person enters or remains unlawfully in a building with intent to commit a crime therein." (ORS 164.215)

So if someone is in your home without your permission and they are there to commit a crime, Oregon law allows you to use deadly force against them. Should you?

While you may be technically obeying the law, any rational person would, if time permits, consider the totality of the circumstances. The court (and public opinion) is going to look far more favorably on a 5'2, 60 year old woman who shoots a 6'1 home invader than they would if you are a healthy 30 year old man who shot an 11 year old who was boosting a video game. Yes, the law is the law, but we saw where that got Sandoval.

Oregon's use of force statutes are copied below. Let me share some opinions that are not legal advice but are born out of many decades on this planet, (none spent as a lawyer), many readings of the rules governing the use of force in the Beaver State, and research with attorneys which I believe summarize the use of force laws in Oregon.

1) Don't start fights.

2) Don't go to places where people like to start fights, especially if they serve booze there.

3) If someone else starts a fight and you can leave, leave.

4) If someone else starts a fight and then changes their mind, let them leave.

5) If someone is taking stuff that doesn't belong to them, do not introduce a firearm into the issue unless you really think they are going to try to hurt you. This is what cell phones and police are for and garden gnomes are not worth the legal bills and possible criminal charges you could face.

6) Do not engage potential adversaries while wearing flip flops.

7) The race is not always to the swift, nor the battle to the strong. But that's the way to bet.

(Ok numbers 6 and 7 have nothing to do with Oregon statutes. I added those for free.)

## USE OF FORCE STATUTES

**161.209 Use of physical force in defense of a person.** Except as provided in ORS 161.215 and 161.219, a person is justified in using physical force upon another person for self-defense or to defend a third person from what the person reasonably believes to be the use or imminent use of unlawful physical force, and the person may use a degree of force which the person reasonably believes to be necessary for the purpose. [1971 c.743 §22]

**161.215 Limitations on use of physical force in defense of a person.** Notwithstanding ORS 161.209, a person is not justified in using physical force upon another person if:

(1) With intent to cause physical injury or death to another person, the person provokes the use of unlawful physical force by that person; or

(2) The person is the initial aggressor, except that the use of physical force upon another person under such circumstances is justifiable if the person withdraws from the encounter and effectively communicates to the other person the intent to do so, but the latter nevertheless continues or threatens to continue the use of unlawful physical force; or

(3) The physical force involved is the product of a combat by agreement not specifically authorized by law. [1971 c.743 §24]

**161.219 Limitations on use of deadly physical force in defense of a person.** Notwithstanding the provisions of ORS 161.209, a person is not justified in using deadly physical force upon another person unless the person reasonably believes that the other person is:

(1) Committing or attempting to commit a felony involving the use or threatened imminent use of physical force against a person; or

(2) Committing or attempting to commit a burglary in a dwelling; or

(3) Using or about to use unlawful deadly physical force against a person. [1971 c.743 §23]

**161.225 Use of physical force in defense of premises.** (1) A person in lawful possession or control of premises is justified in using physical force upon another person when and to the extent that the person reasonably believes it necessary to prevent or terminate what the person reasonably believes to be the commission or attempted commission of a criminal trespass by the other person in or upon the premises.

(2) A person may use deadly physical force under the circumstances set forth in subsection (1) of this section only:

(a) In defense of a person as provided in ORS 161.219; or

(b) When the person reasonably believes it necessary to prevent the commission of arson or a felony by force and violence by the trespasser.

(3) As used in subsection (1) and subsection (2)(a) of this section, "premises" includes any building as defined in ORS 164.205 and any real property. As used in subsection (2)(b) of this section, "premises" includes any building. [1971 c.743 §25]

**161.229 Use of physical force in defense of property.** A person is justified in using physical force, other than deadly physical force, upon another person when and to the extent that the person reasonably believes it to be necessary to prevent or terminate the commission or attempted commission by the other person of theft or criminal mischief of property. [1971 c.743 §26]

# SECTION 13
## RIGHTS RESTORATION

Persons who have lost their firearms rights can have them restored under certain circumstances.

For persons who have disqualifying convictions, one possibility is to seek an expungement. Not all convictions can be expunged. Persons with convictions should check with an attorney in whatever state the conviction took place.

ORS 166.274 describes the other process for seeking firearms rights restoration for persons who are disqualified for criminal convictions and mental health issues.

For persons who are seeking relief after criminal convictions there are a few important things to be aware of before starting the process.

First, there are some crimes that do not allow you to attempt rights restoration under this statute. These follow:

(10) The court may not grant relief under this section to a person who:

(a) Has been convicted of a person felony, as that term is defined in the rules of the Oregon Criminal Justice

Commission, or the statutory counterpart to a person felony in any other jurisdiction, if the offense involved the use of a firearm or a deadly weapon as defined in ORS 161.015;

(b) Has been convicted of an offense listed in ORS 137.700 or the statutory counterpart to an offense listed in ORS 137.700 in any other jurisdiction; or

(c) Is currently serving a felony sentence as defined in ORS 10.030 or has served a felony sentence in the one-year period preceding the filing of the petition.

For persons whose conviction does not bar them from seeking relief, consult ORS 166.274 for the process.

Second, while the Oregon Courts may be able to restore your gun rights after certain felonies, keep in mind that the Feds will not recognize the state's rights restoration immediately. The reason for this is that the Feds do not consider your rights to have been restored until *all* your rights have been restored. To the Feds that means your right to vote, run for office, and *serve on a jury.* Under ORS 10.030 a person may not serve on a jury if that person:

> Has been convicted of a felony or served a felony sentence within the 15 years immediately preceding the date the person is required to report for jury service...

Under ORS 166.274, persons who have lost their rights for mental health issues can apply to have them restored by the Psychiatric Security Review Board.

The Board has created onerous and potentially very expensive requirements for a person to petition for rights restoration. These include demands for all mental health records, some of which may not even exist anymore. This may explain why there have been very, very few cases where the board has actually held the hearing required to restore rights; however in the few cases we know where there have been hearings, all have been successful.

Again, consult ORS 166.274 and the Psychiatric Security Review Board's website for information on this process.

# APPENDIX
## OREGON'S FIREARM STATUTES

### AUTHORITY TO REGULATE FIREARMS

**166.170 State preemption.** (1) Except as expressly authorized by state statute, the authority to regulate in any matter whatsoever the sale, acquisition, transfer, ownership, possession, storage, transportation or use of firearms or any element relating to firearms and components thereof, including ammunition, is vested solely in the Legislative Assembly.

(2) Except as expressly authorized by state statute, no county, city or other municipal corporation or district may enact civil or criminal ordinances, including but not limited to zoning ordinances, to regulate, restrict or prohibit the sale, acquisition, transfer, ownership, possession, storage, transportation or use of firearms or any element relating to firearms and components thereof, including ammunition. Ordinances that are contrary to this subsection are void. [1995 s.s. c.1 §1]

**166.171 Authority of county to regulate discharge of firearms.** (1) A county may adopt ordinances to regulate, restrict or prohibit the discharge of firearms within their boundaries.

(2) Ordinances adopted under subsection (1) of this section may not apply to or affect:

(a) A person discharging a firearm in the lawful defense of person or property.

(b) A person discharging a firearm in the course of lawful hunting.

(c) A landowner and guests of the landowner discharging a firearm, when the discharge will not endanger adjacent persons or property.

(d) A person discharging a firearm on a public or private shooting range, shooting gallery or other area designed and built for the purpose of target shooting.

(e) A person discharging a firearm in the course of target shooting on public land that is not inside an urban growth boundary or the boundary of a city, if the discharge will not endanger persons or property.

(f) An employee of the United States Department of Agriculture, acting within the scope of employment, discharging a firearm in the course of the lawful taking of wildlife. [1995 s.s. c.1 §2; 2009 c.556 §1]

**166.172 Authority of city to regulate discharge of firearms.** (1) A city may adopt ordinances to regulate, restrict or prohibit the discharge of firearms within the city's boundaries.

(2) Ordinances adopted under subsection (1) of this section may not apply to or affect:

(a) A person discharging a firearm in the lawful defense of person or property.

(b) A person discharging a firearm on a public or private shooting range, shooting gallery or other area designed and built for the purpose of target shooting.

(c) An employee of the United States Department of Agriculture, acting within the scope of employment, discharging a firearm in the course of the lawful taking of wildlife. [1995 s.s. c.1 §3; 2009 c.556 §2]

**166.173 Authority of city or county to regulate possession of loaded firearms in public places.** (1) A city or county may adopt ordinances to regulate, restrict or prohibit the possession of loaded firearms in public places as defined in ORS 161.015.

(2) Ordinances adopted under subsection (1) of this section do not apply to or affect:

(a) A law enforcement officer.

(b) A member of the military in the performance of official duty.

(c) A person licensed to carry a concealed handgun.

(d) A person authorized to possess a loaded firearm while in or on a public building or court facility under ORS 166.370.

(e) An employee of the United States Department of Agriculture, acting within the scope of employment, who possesses a loaded firearm in the course of the lawful taking of wildlife.

(f) An honorably retired law enforcement officer, unless the person who is a retired law enforcement officer has been convicted of an offense that would make the person ineligible to obtain a concealed handgun license under ORS 166.291 and 166.292. [1995 s.s. c.1 §4; 1999 c.782 §8; 2009 c.556 §3; 2015 c.709 §1]

**166.174 Authority of city, county, municipal corporation or district to regulate possession or sale of firearms.** Notwithstanding any other provision of law, a city, county or other municipal corporation or district may not adopt ordinances that regulate, restrict or prohibit the possession or sale of firearms in a public building that is rented or leased to a person during the term of the lease. [1995 s.s. c.1 §5]

**166.175 Authority of city to regulate purchase of used firearms.** (1) Notwithstanding any other provision of law, a city may continue to regulate the purchase of used firearms by pawnshops and secondhand stores.

(2) As used in this section, "secondhand store" means a store or business whose primary source of revenue is the sale of used merchandise. [1995 s.s. c.1 §6]

**166.176 Exception to preemption for certain county ordinances.** (1) Nothing in ORS 166.170 or 166.171 is intended to preempt, invalidate or in any way affect the operation of any provision of a county ordinance that was in effect on November 2, 1995, to the extent that the provision:

(a) Established a procedure for regulating, restricting or prohibiting the discharge of firearms; or

(b) Regulated, restricted or prohibited the discharge of firearms.

(2) Subsection (1) of this section does not apply to:

(a) Ordinances regulating, restricting or prohibiting the discharge of firearms on a shooting range or in a shooting gallery or other area designed and built for the purpose of target shooting.

(b) An employee of the United States Department of Agriculture, acting within the scope of employment, discharging a firearm in the course of the lawful taking of wildlife. [1997 c.403 §1; 2009 c.556 §4]

## POSSESSION AND USE OF WEAPONS

**166.180 Negligently wounding another.** Any person who, as a result of failure to use ordinary care under the circumstances, wounds any other person with a bullet or shot from any firearm, or with an arrow from any bow, commits a Class B misdemeanor. In addition, any person so convicted shall forfeit any license to hunt, obtained under the laws of this state, and shall be ineligible to obtain a license to hunt for a period of 10 years following the date of conviction. [Formerly 163.310; 2011 c.597 §162]

**166.190 Pointing firearm at another; courts having jurisdiction over offense.** Any person over the age of 12 years who, with or without malice, purposely points or aims any loaded or empty pistol, gun, revolver or other firearm, at or toward any other person within range of the firearm, except in self-defense, shall be fined upon conviction in any sum not less than $10 nor more than $500, or be imprisoned in the county jail not less than 10 days nor more than six months, or both. Justice courts have jurisdiction concurrent with the circuit court of the trial of violations of this section. When any person is charged before a justice court with violation of this section, the court shall, upon motion of the district attorney, at any time before trial, act as a committing magistrate, and if probable cause be established, hold such person to the grand jury. [Formerly 163.320]

**166.210 Definitions.** As used in ORS 166.250 to 166.270, 166.291 to 166.295 and 166.410 to 166.470:

(1) "Antique firearm" means:

(a) Any firearm, including any firearm with a matchlock, flintlock, percussion cap or similar type of ignition system, manufactured in or before 1898; and

(b) Any replica of any firearm described in paragraph (a) of this subsection if the replica:

(A) Is not designed or redesigned for using rimfire or conventional centerfire fixed ammunition; or

(B) Uses rimfire or conventional centerfire fixed ammunition that is no longer manufactured in the United States and that is not readily available in the ordinary channels of commercial trade.

(2) "Corrections officer" has the meaning given that term in ORS 181A.355.

(3) "Firearm" means a weapon, by whatever name known, which is designed to expel a projectile by the action of powder.

(4) "Firearms silencer" means any device for silencing, muffling or diminishing the report of a firearm.

(5) "Handgun" means any pistol or revolver using a fixed cartridge containing a propellant charge, primer and projectile, and designed to be aimed or fired otherwise than from the shoulder.

(6) "Machine gun" means a weapon of any description by whatever name known, loaded or unloaded, which is designed or modified to allow two or more shots to be fired by a single pressure on the trigger device.

(7) "Minor" means a person under 18 years of age.

(8) "Offense" has the meaning given that term in ORS 161.505.

(9) "Parole and probation officer" has the meaning given that term in ORS 181A.355.

(10) "Peace officer" has the meaning given that term in ORS 133.005.

(11) "Short-barreled rifle" means a rifle having one or more barrels less than 16 inches in length and any weapon made from a rifle if the weapon has an overall length of less than 26 inches.

(12) "Short-barreled shotgun" means a shotgun having one or more barrels less than 18 inches in length and any weapon made from a shotgun if the weapon has an overall length of less than 26 inches. [Amended by 1977 c.769 §1; 1979 c.779 §3; 1989 c.839 §1; 1993 c.735 §14; 1995 c.670 §3; 1999 c.1040 §2; 2001 c.666 §§32,44; 2003 c.614 §7; 2007 c.368 §1; 2009 c.610 §4]

**166.220 Unlawful use of weapon.** (1) A person commits the crime of unlawful use of a weapon if the person:

(a) Attempts to use unlawfully against another, or carries or possesses with intent to use unlawfully against another, any dangerous or deadly weapon as defined in ORS 161.015; or

(b) Intentionally discharges a firearm, blowgun, bow and arrow, crossbow or explosive device within the city limits of any city or within residential areas within urban growth boundaries at or in the direction of any person, building, structure or vehicle within the range of the weapon without having legal authority for such discharge.

(2) This section does not apply to:

(a) Police officers or military personnel in the lawful performance of their official duties;

(b) Persons lawfully defending life or property as provided in ORS 161.219;

(c) Persons discharging firearms, blowguns, bows and arrows, crossbows or explosive devices upon public or private shooting ranges, shooting galleries or other areas designated and built for the purpose of target shooting;

(d) Persons lawfully engaged in hunting in compliance with rules and regulations adopted by the State Department of Fish and Wildlife; or

(e) An employee of the United States Department of Agriculture, acting within the scope of employment, discharging a firearm in the course of the lawful taking of wildlife.

(3) Unlawful use of a weapon is a Class C felony. [Amended by 1975 c.700 §1; 1985 c.543 §1; 1991 c.797 §1; 2009 c.556 §5]

**166.230** [Repealed by 1979 c.779 §7]

**166.240 Carrying of concealed weapons.** (1) Except as provided in subsection (2) of this section, any person who carries concealed upon the person any knife having a blade that projects or swings into position by force of a spring or by centrifugal force, any dirk, dagger, ice pick, slungshot, metal knuckles, or any similar instrument by the use of which injury could be inflicted upon the person or property of any other person, commits a Class B misdemeanor.

(2) Nothing in subsection (1) of this section applies to any peace officer as defined in ORS 133.005, whose duty it is to serve process or make arrests. Justice courts have concurrent jurisdiction to try any person charged with violating any of the provisions of subsection (1) of this section. [Amended by 1977 c.454 §1; 1985 c.543 §2; 1989 c.839 §21; 1999 c.1040 §15]

**166.245 [1989 c.839 §38; repealed by 1995 s.s. c.1 §7]**

**166.250 Unlawful possession of firearms.** (1) Except as otherwise provided in this section or ORS 166.260, 166.270, 166.273, 166.274, 166.291, 166.292 or 166.410 to 166.470, a person commits the crime of unlawful possession of a firearm if the person knowingly:

(a) Carries any firearm concealed upon the person;

(b) Possesses a handgun that is concealed and readily accessible to the person within any vehicle; or

(c) Possesses a firearm and:

(A) Is under 18 years of age;

(B)(i) While a minor, was found to be within the jurisdiction of the juvenile court for having committed an act which, if committed by an adult, would constitute a felony or a misdemeanor involving violence, as defined in ORS 166.470; and

(ii) Was discharged from the jurisdiction of the juvenile court within four years prior to being charged under this section;

(C) Has been convicted of a felony;

(D) Was committed to the Oregon Health Authority under ORS 426.130;

(E) Was found to be a person with mental illness and subject to an order under ORS 426.130 that the person be prohibited from purchasing or possessing a firearm as a result of that mental illness;

(F) Is presently subject to an order under ORS 426.133 prohibiting the person from purchasing or possessing a firearm;

(G) Has been found guilty except for insanity under ORS 161.295 of a felony; or

(H) The possession of the firearm by the person is prohibited under ORS 166.255.

(2) This section does not prohibit:

(a) A minor, who is not otherwise prohibited under subsection (1)(c) of this section, from possessing a firearm:

(A) Other than a handgun, if the firearm was transferred to the minor by the minor's parent or guardian or by another person with the consent of the minor's parent or guardian; or

(B) Temporarily for hunting, target practice or any other lawful purpose; or

(b) Any citizen of the United States over the age of 18 years who resides in or is temporarily sojourning within this state, and who is not within the excepted classes prescribed by ORS 166.270 and subsection (1) of this section, from owning, possessing or keeping within the person's place of residence or place of business any handgun, and no permit or license to purchase, own, possess or keep any such firearm at the person's place of residence or place of business is required of any such citizen. As used in this subsection, "residence" includes a recreational vessel or recreational vehicle while used, for whatever period of time, as residential quarters.

(3) Firearms carried openly in belt holsters are not concealed within the meaning of this section.

(4)(a) Except as provided in paragraphs (b) and (c) of this subsection, a handgun is readily accessible within the meaning of this section if the handgun is within the passenger compartment of the vehicle.

(b) If a vehicle, other than a vehicle described in paragraph (c) of this subsection, has no storage location that is outside the passenger compartment of the vehicle, a handgun is not readily accessible within the meaning of this section if:

(A) The handgun is stored in a closed and locked glove compartment, center console or other container; and

(B) The key is not inserted into the lock, if the glove compartment, center console or other container unlocks with a key.

(c) If the vehicle is a motorcycle, an all-terrain vehicle or a snowmobile, a handgun is not readily accessible within the meaning of this section if:

(A) The handgun is in a locked container within or affixed to the vehicle; or

(B) The handgun is equipped with a trigger lock or other locking mechanism that prevents the discharge of the firearm.

(5) Unlawful possession of a firearm is a Class A misdemeanor. [Amended by 1979 c.779 §4; 1985 c.543 §3; 1989 c.839 §13; 1993 c.732 §1; 1993 c.735 §12; 1999 c.1040 §1; 2001 c.666 §§33,45; 2003 c.614 §8; 2009 c.499 §1; 2009 c.595 §112; 2009 c.826 §§8a,11a; 2011 c.662 §§1,2; 2013 c.360 §§6,7; 2015 c.50 §§12,13; 2015 c.201 §3; 2015 c.497 §§3,4]

**166.255 Possession of firearm or ammunition by certain persons prohibited.** (1) It is unlawful for a person to knowingly possess a firearm or ammunition if:

(a) The person is the subject of a court order that:

(A) Was issued or continued after a hearing for which the person had actual notice and during the course of which the person had an opportunity to be heard;

(B) Restrains the person from stalking, intimidating, molesting or menacing an intimate partner, a child of an intimate partner or a child of the person; and

(C) Includes a finding that the person represents a credible threat to the physical safety of an intimate partner, a child of an intimate partner or a child of the person; or

(b) The person has been convicted of a qualifying misdemeanor and, at the time of the offense, the person was a family member of the victim of the offense.

(2) The prohibition described in subsection (1)(a) of this section does not apply with respect to the transportation, shipment, receipt, possession or importation of any firearm or ammunition

imported for, sold or shipped to or issued for the use of the United States Government or any federal department or agency, or any state or department, agency or political subdivision of a state.

(3) As used in this section:

(a) "Convicted" means:

(A) The person was represented by counsel or knowingly and intelligently waived the right to counsel;

(B) The case was tried to a jury, if the crime was one for which the person was entitled to a jury trial, or the person knowingly and intelligently waived the person's right to a jury trial; and

(C) The conviction has not been set aside or expunged, and the person has not been pardoned.

(b) "Deadly weapon" has the meaning given that term in ORS 161.015.

(c) "Family member" means, with respect to the victim, the victim's spouse, the victim's former spouse, a person with whom the victim shares a child in common, the victim's parent or guardian, a person cohabiting with or who has cohabited with the victim as a spouse, parent or guardian or a person similarly situated to a spouse, parent or guardian of the victim.

(d) "Intimate partner" means, with respect to a person, the person's spouse, the person's former spouse, a parent of the person's child or another person who has cohabited or is cohabiting with the person in a relationship akin to a spouse.

(e) "Possess" has the meaning given that term in ORS 161.015.

(f) "Qualifying misdemeanor" means a misdemeanor that has, as an element of the offense, the use or attempted use of physical force or the threatened use of a deadly weapon. [2015 c.497 §2]

**166.260 Persons not affected by ORS 166.250.** (1) ORS 166.250 does not apply to or affect:

(a) A parole and probation officer, police officer or reserve officer, as those terms are defined in ORS 181A.355.

(b) A federal officer, as defined in ORS 133.005, or a certified reserve officer or corrections officer, as those terms are defined in ORS 181A.355, while the federal officer, certified reserve officer or corrections officer is acting within the scope of employment.

(c) An honorably retired law enforcement officer, unless the person who is a retired law enforcement officer has been convicted of an offense that would make the person ineligible to obtain a concealed handgun license under ORS 166.291 and 166.292.

(d) Any person summoned by an officer described in paragraph (a) or (b) of this subsection to assist in making arrests or preserving the peace, while the summoned person is engaged in assisting the officer.

(e) The possession or transportation by any merchant of unloaded firearms as merchandise.

(f) Active or reserve members of:

(A) The Army, Navy, Air Force, Coast Guard or Marine Corps of the United States, or of the National Guard, when on duty;

(B) The commissioned corps of the National Oceanic and Atmospheric Administration; or

(C) The Public Health Service of the United States Department of Health and Human Services, when detailed by proper authority for duty with the Army or Navy of the United States.

(g) Organizations which are by law authorized to purchase or receive weapons described in ORS 166.250 from the United States, or from this state.

(h) Duly authorized military or civil organizations while parading, or the members thereof when going to and from the places of meeting of their organization.

(i) A person who is licensed under ORS 166.291 and 166.292 to carry a concealed handgun.

(2) It is an affirmative defense to a charge of violating ORS 166.250 (1)(c)(C) that the person has been granted relief from the disability under ORS 166.274.

(3) Except for persons who are otherwise prohibited from possessing a firearm under ORS 166.250 (1)(c) or 166.270, ORS 166.250 does not apply to or affect:

(a) Members of any club or organization, for the purpose of practicing shooting at targets upon the established target ranges, whether public or private, while such members are using any of the firearms referred to in ORS 166.250 upon such target ranges, or while going to and from such ranges.

(b) Licensed hunters or fishermen while engaged in hunting or fishing, or while going to or returning from a hunting or fishing expedition.

(4) The exceptions listed in subsection (1)(d) to (i) of this section constitute affirmative defenses to a charge of violating ORS 166.250. [Amended by 1977 c.207 §1; 1991 c.67 §36; 1993 c.735 §1; 1995 c.670 §2; 1999 c.1040 §3; 2009 c.316 §2; 2009 c.499 §4; 2012 c.106 §3; 2015 c.709 §2]

**166.262 Limitation on peace officer's authority to arrest for violating ORS 166.250 or 166.370.** A peace officer may not arrest or charge a person for violating ORS 166.250 (1)(a) or (b) or 166.370 (1) if the person has in the person's immediate possession:

(1) A valid license to carry a firearm as provided in ORS 166.291 and 166.292;

(2) Proof that the person is a law enforcement officer; or

(3) Proof that the person is an honorably retired law enforcement officer, unless the person has been convicted of an offense that would make the person ineligible to obtain a concealed handgun license under ORS 166.291 and 166.292. [1999 c.1040 §5; 2015 c.709 §3]

**166.263 Authority of parole and probation officer to carry firearm.** When authorized by the officer's employer, a parole and probation officer, as defined in ORS 181A.355, may carry a firearm while engaged in official duties if the officer has completed:

(1) A firearms training program recognized by the Board on Public Safety Standards and Training; and

(2) A psychological screening. [1995 c.670 §1]

**166.270 Possession of weapons by certain felons.** (1) Any person who has been convicted of a felony under the law of this state or any other state, or who has been convicted of a felony under the laws of the Government of the United States, who owns or has in the person's possession or under the person's custody or control any firearm commits the crime of felon in possession of a firearm.

(2) Any person who has been convicted of a felony under the law of this state or any other state, or who has been convicted of a felony under the laws of the Government of the United States, who owns or has in the person's possession or under the person's custody or control any instrument or weapon having a blade that projects or swings into position by force of a spring or by centrifugal force or any blackjack, slungshot, sandclub, sandbag, sap glove, metal knuckles or an Electro-Muscular Disruption Technology device as defined in ORS 165.540, or who carries a dirk, dagger or stiletto, commits the crime of felon in possession of a restricted weapon.

(3) For the purposes of this section, a person "has been convicted of a felony" if, at the time of conviction for an offense, that offense was a felony under the law of the jurisdiction in which it was committed. Such conviction shall not be deemed a conviction of a felony if:

(a) The court declared the conviction to be a misdemeanor at the time of judgment; or

(b) The offense was possession of marijuana and the conviction was prior to January 1, 1972.

(4) Subsection (1) of this section does not apply to any person who has been:

(a) Convicted of only one felony under the law of this state or any other state, or who has been convicted of only one felony under the laws of the United States, which felony did not involve criminal homicide, as defined in ORS 163.005, or the possession or use of a firearm or a weapon having a blade that projects or swings into position by force of a spring or by centrifugal force, and who has been discharged from imprisonment, parole or probation for said offense for a period of 15 years prior to the date of alleged violation of subsection (1) of this section; or

(b) Granted relief from the disability under 18 U.S.C. 925(c) or ORS 166.274 or has had the person's record expunged under the laws of this state or equivalent laws of another jurisdiction.

(5) Felon in possession of a firearm is a Class C felony. Felon in possession of a restricted weapon is a Class A misdemeanor. [Amended by 1975 c.702 §1; 1985 c.543 §4; 1985 c.709 §2; 1987 c.853 §1; 1989 c.839 §4; 1993 c.735 §2; 1995 c.518 §1; 1999 c.1040 §16; 2003 c.14 §64; 2009 c.189 §1; 2009 c.499 §3]

**166.272 Unlawful possession of machine guns, certain short-barreled firearms and firearms silencers.** (1) A person commits the crime of unlawful possession of a machine gun, short-barreled rifle, short-barreled shotgun or firearms silencer if the person knowingly possesses any machine gun, short-barreled rifle, short-barreled shotgun or firearms silencer.

(2) Unlawful possession of a machine gun, short-barreled rifle, short-barreled shotgun or firearms silencer is a Class B felony.

(3) A peace officer may not arrest or charge a person for violating subsection (1) of this section if the person has in the person's immediate possession documentation showing that the machine gun, short-barreled rifle, short-barreled shotgun or firearms silencer is registered as required under federal law.

(4) It is an affirmative defense to a charge of violating subsection (1) of this section that the machine gun, short-barreled rifle, short-barreled shotgun or firearms silencer was registered as required under federal law. [1989 c.839 §13a; 1997 c.749 §8; 1997 c.798 §1]

**166.273 Relief from firearm prohibitions related to mental health.**
(1) A person barred from transporting, shipping, possessing or receiving a firearm may file a petition with the Psychiatric Security Review Board for relief from the bar if:

(a) The person is barred from possessing a firearm under ORS 166.250 (1)(c)(D) or (E);

(b) The person is barred from receiving a firearm under ORS 166.470 (1)(e) or (f) or, if the person has been found guilty except for insanity of a misdemeanor involving violence, ORS 166.470 (1)(g); or

(c) The person is barred from possessing, receiving, shipping or transporting a firearm under 18 U.S.C. 922(d)(4) or (g)(4) as the result of a state mental health determination.

(2) The petitioner shall serve a copy of the petition on:

(a) The Department of Human Services and the Oregon Health Authority; and

(b) The district attorney in each county in which:

(A) The person was committed by a court to the Oregon Health Authority, or adjudicated by a court as a person with mental illness, under ORS 426.130;

(B) The person was committed by a court to the Department of Human Services, or adjudicated by a court as in need of commitment for residential care, treatment and training, under ORS 427.290;

(C) The person was found guilty except for insanity under ORS 161.295;

(D) The person was found responsible except for insanity under ORS 419C.411; or

(E) The person was found by a court to lack fitness to proceed under ORS 161.370.

(3) Following receipt of the petition, the board shall conduct a contested case hearing, make written findings of fact and conclusions of law on the issues before the board and issue a final order. Board members from the adult panel, the juvenile panel or a combination of both panels of the board may conduct the hearings described in this section.

(4) The state and any person or entity described in subsection (2) of this section may appear and object to and present evidence relevant to the relief sought by the petitioner.

(5) The board shall grant the relief requested in the petition if the petitioner demonstrates, based on the petitioner's reputation, the petitioner's record, the circumstances surrounding the firearm disability and any other evidence in the record, that the petitioner will not be likely to act in a manner that is dangerous to public safety and that granting the relief would not be contrary to the public interest.

(6) If the board grants the relief requested in the petition, the board shall provide to the Department of State Police the minimum information necessary, as defined in ORS 181A.290, to enable the department to:

(a) Maintain the information and transmit the information to the federal government as required under federal law; and

(b) Maintain a record of the person's relief from the disqualification to possess or receive a firearm under ORS 166.250 (1)(c)(D) or (E) or 166.470 (1)(e), (f) or (g).

(7) The petitioner may petition for judicial review of a final order of the board. The petition shall be filed in the circuit court of a county described in subsection (2)(b) of this section. The review shall be conducted de novo and without a jury.

(8) A petitioner may take an appeal from the circuit court to the Court of Appeals. Review by the Court of Appeals shall be conducted in accordance with ORS 183.500.

(9) A person may file a petition for relief under this section no more than once every two years.

(10) The board shall adopt procedural rules to carry out the provisions of this section.

(11) As used in this section, "state mental health determination" means:

(a) A finding by a court that a person lacks fitness to proceed under ORS 161.370;

(b) A finding that a person is guilty except for insanity of a crime under ORS 161.295 or responsible except for insanity of an act under ORS 419C.411 or any determination by the Psychiatric Security Review Board thereafter;

(c) A commitment by a court to the Oregon Health Authority, or an adjudication by a court that a person is a person with mental illness, under ORS 426.130; or

(d) A commitment by a court to the Department of Human Services, or an adjudication by a court that a person is in need of commitment for residential care, treatment and training, under ORS 427.290. [2009 c.826 §5; 2009 c.826 §§18,18a; 2011 c.658 §32; 2013 c.360 §68; 2015 c.201 §2]

**166.274 Relief from prohibition against possessing or receiving firearm; fees.** (1) Except as provided in subsection (11) of this section, a person barred from possessing or receiving a firearm may file a petition for relief from the bar in accordance with subsection (2) of this section if:

    (a) The person is barred from possessing a firearm under ORS 166.250 (1)(c)(A), (C) or (H) or 166.270; or

    (b) The person is barred from receiving a firearm under ORS 166.470 (1)(a) or (b) or, if the person has been convicted of a misdemeanor involving violence, ORS 166.470 (1)(g).

(2) A petition for relief described in this section must be filed in the circuit court in the petitioner's county of residence.

(3) A person may apply once per calendar year for relief under the provisions of this section.

(4)(a) A person petitioning for relief under this section shall serve a copy of the petition on:

    (A) The city chief of police if the court in which the petition is filed is located in a city; or

    (B) The sheriff of the county in which the court is located.

    (b) The copy of the petition shall be served on the chief of police or sheriff at the same time the petition is filed at the court.

(5)(a) When a petition is denied, the judge shall cause that information to be entered into the Department of State Police computerized criminal history files.

    (b) When a petition is granted, the judge shall cause that information and a fingerprint card of the petitioner to be entered into the Department of State Police computerized criminal history files. If, after a petition is granted, the petitioner is arrested and convicted of a crime that would disqualify the petitioner from purchasing or possessing a firearm, the Department of State Police shall notify the court that granted relief under this section. The court shall review the order granting relief and determine whether to rescind the order. The Department of State Police may charge a reasonable fee, under ORS 192.440, for the entry and maintenance of information under this section.

(6) Notwithstanding the provisions of ORS 9.320, a party that is not a natural person, the state or any city, county, district or other political subdivision or public corporation in this state, without

appearance by attorney, may appear as a party to an action under this section.

(7) If the petitioner seeks relief from the bar on possessing or purchasing a firearm, relief shall be granted when the petitioner demonstrates, by clear and convincing evidence, that the petitioner does not pose a threat to the safety of the public or the petitioner.

(8) Petitions filed under this section shall be heard and disposed of within 15 judicial days of filing or as soon as is practicable thereafter, but not more than 30 days thereafter. The judge shall then make findings and conclusions and issue a judgment based on the findings and conclusions in accordance with the requirements of law.

(9) A person filing a petition under this section must pay the filing fee established under ORS 21.135.

(10)(a) Initial appeals of petitions shall be heard de novo.

(b) Any party to a judgment under this subsection may appeal to the Court of Appeals in the same manner as for any other civil action.

(c) If the governmental entity files an appeal under this subsection and does not prevail, it shall be ordered to pay the attorney fees for the prevailing party.

(11) The court may not grant relief under this section to a person who:

(a) Has been convicted of a person felony, as that term is defined in the rules of the Oregon Criminal Justice Commission, or the statutory counterpart to a person felony in any other jurisdiction, if the offense involved the use of a firearm or a deadly weapon as defined in ORS 161.015;

(b) Has been convicted of an offense listed in ORS 137.700 or the statutory counterpart to an offense listed in ORS 137.700 in any other jurisdiction; or

(c) Is currently serving a felony sentence as defined in ORS 10.030 or has served a felony sentence in the one-year period preceding the filing of the petition. [1989 c.839 §11; 1991 c.67 §37; 1993 c.732 §§3,4; 1995 c.518 §2; 1995 c.658 §88; 2009 c.499 §2; 2009 c.826 §§19,20; 2010 c.86 §§1,2,3; 2011 c.595 §§59,60; 2011 c.662 §§3,4; 2015 c.7 §§6,7; 2015 c.201 §4; 2015 c.497 §§5,6]

**166.275 Possession of weapons by inmates of institutions.** Any person committed to any institution who, while under the jurisdiction of any institution or while being conveyed to or from any institution, possesses or carries upon the person, or has under the custody or control of the person any dangerous instrument, or any weapon including but not limited to any blackjack, slingshot, billy, sand club, metal knuckles, explosive substance, dirk, dagger, sharp instrument, pistol, revolver or other firearm without lawful authority, is guilty of a felony and upon conviction thereof shall be punished by imprisonment in the custody of the Department of Corrections for a term not more than 20 years. [1953 c.533 §1; 1987 c.320 §88]

**166.279 Forfeiture of deadly weapons.** (1) Except as provided in subsection (4) of this section, ORS 131.550 to 131.600 do not apply to the forfeiture of a firearm or other deadly weapon that was possessed, used or available for use to facilitate a criminal offense.

(2) Except as provided in subsection (3) of this section, at the time of sentencing for any criminal offense in which a firearm or other deadly weapon was possessed, used or available for use to facilitate the offense, the court shall declare the weapon to be contraband and order that the weapon be forfeited.

(3) If a firearm or other deadly weapon that was possessed, used or available for use to facilitate a criminal offense was stolen from its lawful owner and was recovered from a person other than the lawful owner, the court may not order that the weapon be forfeited but shall order that the weapon be restored to the lawful owner as soon as the weapon is no longer needed for evidentiary purposes.

(4) The court shall release a firearm or other deadly weapon forfeited under subsection (2) of this section to the law enforcement agency that seized the weapon. The law enforcement agency may destroy or sell the weapon, use the weapon as a service weapon or use the weapon for training, identification or demonstration purposes. When a weapon is sold pursuant to this subsection, the law enforcement agency shall pay the proceeds from the sale, less the costs of the sale, as provided in ORS 131.594 and 131.597.

(5) As used in this section, "deadly weapon" has the meaning given that term in ORS 161.015. [2003 c.614 §4; 2005 c.830 §24]

**166.280** [Amended by 1981 c.767 §1; 1993 c.625 §2; 1997 c.480 §5; 1997 c.693 §2; repealed by 2001 c.666 §56]

**166.281** [2001 c.666 §52; repealed by 2003 c.614 §13]

**166.282 Sale of weapons by political subdivision; disposition of proceeds.** (1) A political subdivision in this state that sells a weapon described in subsection (2) of this section shall pay the proceeds from the sale of the weapon, less the costs of the sale, to the account of the police agency that received the weapon, to be used for purposes of public safety, law enforcement and crime prevention and detection.

(2) Subsection (1) of this section applies to a weapon that is donated to the police agency. [1997 c.693 §1; 2001 c.666 §§25,37; 2003 c.614 §5]

**166.290** [Amended by 1973 c.391 §1; repealed by 1989 c.839 §7 (166.291 to 166.293 enacted in lieu of 166.290)]

**166.291 Issuance of concealed handgun license; application; fees; liability.** (1) The sheriff of a county, upon a person's application for an Oregon concealed handgun license, upon receipt of the appropriate fees and after compliance with the procedures set out in this section, shall issue the person a concealed handgun license if the person:

(a)(A) Is a citizen of the United States; or

(B) Is a legal resident alien who can document continuous residency in the county for at least six months and has declared in writing to the United States Citizenship and Immigration Services the intent to acquire citizenship status and can present proof of the written declaration to the sheriff at the time of application for the license;

(b) Is at least 21 years of age;

(c) Is a resident of the county;

(d) Has no outstanding warrants for arrest;

(e) Is not free on any form of pretrial release;

(f) Demonstrates competence with a handgun by any one of the following:

(A) Completion of any hunter education or hunter safety course approved by the State Department of Fish and Wildlife or a similar agency of another state if handgun safety was a component of the course;

(B) Completion of any National Rifle Association firearms safety or training course if handgun safety was a component of the course;

(C) Completion of any firearms safety or training course or class available to the general public offered by law enforcement, community college, or private or public institution or organization or firearms training school utilizing instructors certified by the National Rifle Association or a law enforcement agency if handgun safety was a component of the course;

(D) Completion of any law enforcement firearms safety or training course or class offered for security guards, investigators, reserve law enforcement officers or any other law enforcement officers if handgun safety was a component of the course;

(E) Presents evidence of equivalent experience with a handgun through participation in organized shooting competition or military service;

(F) Is licensed or has been licensed to carry a firearm in this state, unless the license has been revoked; or

(G) Completion of any firearms training or safety course or class conducted by a firearms instructor certified by a law enforcement agency or the National Rifle Association if handgun safety was a component of the course;

(g) Has never been convicted of a felony or found guilty, except for insanity under ORS 161.295, of a felony;

(h) Has not been convicted of a misdemeanor or found guilty, except for insanity under ORS 161.295, of a misdemeanor within the four years prior to the application, including a misdemeanor conviction for the possession of marijuana as described in paragraph (L) of this subsection;

(i) Has not been committed to the Oregon Health Authority under ORS 426.130;

(j) Has not been found to be a person with mental illness and is not subject to an order under ORS 426.130 that the person be prohibited from purchasing or possessing a firearm as a result of that mental illness;

(k) Has been discharged from the jurisdiction of the juvenile court for more than four years if, while a minor, the person was found to be within the jurisdiction of the juvenile court for having committed an act that, if committed by an adult, would constitute a felony or a misdemeanor involving violence, as defined in ORS 166.470;

(L) Has not been convicted of an offense involving controlled substances or participated in a court-supervised drug diversion program, except this disability does not operate to exclude a person if:

(A) The person can demonstrate that the person has been convicted only once of a marijuana possession offense that constituted a misdemeanor or violation under the law of the jurisdiction of the offense, and has not completed a drug diversion program for a marijuana possession offense that constituted a misdemeanor or violation under the law of the jurisdiction of the offense; or

(B) The person can demonstrate that the person has only once completed a drug diversion program for a marijuana possession offense that constituted a misdemeanor or violation under the law of the jurisdiction of the offense, and has not been convicted of a marijuana possession offense that constituted a misdemeanor or violation under the law of the jurisdiction of the offense;

(m) Is not subject to a citation issued under ORS 163.735 or an order issued under ORS 30.866, 107.700 to 107.735 or 163.738;

(n) Has not received a dishonorable discharge from the Armed Forces of the United States;

(o) Is not required to register as a sex offender in any state; and

(p) Is not presently subject to an order under ORS 426.133 prohibiting the person from purchasing or possessing a firearm.

(2) A person who has been granted relief under ORS 166.273, 166.274 or 166.293 or 18 U.S.C. 925(c) or has had the person's record expunged under the laws of this state or equivalent laws of other jurisdictions is not subject to the disabilities in subsection (1) (g) to (L) of this section.

(3) Before the sheriff may issue a license:

(a) The application must state the applicant's legal name, current address and telephone number, date and place of birth, hair and eye color and height and weight. The application must also list the applicant's residence address or addresses for the previous three years. The application must contain a statement by the applicant that the applicant meets the requirements of subsection (1) of this section. The application may include the Social Security number of the applicant if the applicant voluntarily provides this number. The application must be signed by the applicant.

(b) The applicant must submit to fingerprinting and photographing by the sheriff. The sheriff shall fingerprint and photograph the applicant and shall conduct any investigation necessary to corroborate the requirements listed under subsection (1) of this section. If a nationwide criminal records check is necessary, the sheriff shall request the Department of State Police to conduct the check, including fingerprint identification, through the Federal Bureau of Investigation. The Federal Bureau of Investigation shall return the fingerprint cards used to conduct the criminal records check and may not keep any record of the fingerprints. The Department of State Police shall report the results of the fingerprint-based criminal records check to the sheriff. The Department of State Police shall also furnish the sheriff with any information about the applicant that the Department of State Police may have in its possession including, but not limited to, manual or computerized criminal offender information.

(4) Application forms for concealed handgun licenses shall be supplied by the sheriff upon request. The forms shall be uniform throughout this state in substantially the following form:

---

APPLICATION FOR LICENSE TO CARRY CONCEALED HANDGUN

Date_____

I hereby declare as follows:

I am a citizen of the United States or a legal resident alien who can document continuous residency in the county for at least six months and have declared in writing to the United States Citizenship and Immigration Services my intention to become a citizen and can present proof of the written declaration to the sheriff at the time of this application. I am at least 21 years of age. I have been discharged from the jurisdiction of the juvenile court for more than four years if, while a minor, I was found to be within the jurisdiction of the juvenile court for having committed an act that, if committed by an adult, would constitute a felony or a misdemeanor involving violence, as defined in ORS 166.470. I have never been convicted of a felony or found guilty, except for insanity under ORS 161.295, of a felony in the State of Oregon or elsewhere. I have not, within the last four years, been convicted of a misdemeanor or found guilty, except for insanity under ORS 161.295, of a misdemeanor. Except as provided in ORS 166.291 (1)(L), I have not been convicted of an offense involving controlled substances or completed a court-supervised drug diversion program. There are no outstanding warrants for my arrest and I am not free on any form of pretrial release. I have not been committed to the Oregon Health Authority under ORS 426.130, nor have I been found to be a person with mental illness and presently subject to an order prohibiting me from purchasing or possessing a firearm because of mental illness. I am not under a court order to participate in assisted outpatient treatment that includes an order prohibiting me from purchasing or possessing a firearm. If any of the previous conditions do apply to me, I have been granted relief or wish to petition for relief from the disability under ORS 166.273, 166.274 or 166.293 or 18 U.S.C. 925(c) or have had the records expunged. I am not subject to a citation issued under ORS 163.735 or an order issued under ORS 30.866, 107.700 to 107.735 or 163.738. I have never received a dishonorable discharge from the Armed Forces of the United States. I am not required to register as a sex offender in any state. I understand I will be fingerprinted and photographed.

Legal name _____

Age _____ Date of birth _____

Place of birth _____

Social Security number _____

(Disclosure of your Social Security account number is voluntary. Solicitation of the number is authorized under ORS 166.291. It will be used only as a means of identification.)

Proof of identification (Two pieces of current identification are required, one of which must bear a photograph of the applicant. The type of identification and the number on the identification are to be filled in by the sheriff.):

     1._____

     2._____

Height _____ Weight _____

Hair color _____ Eye color _____

Current address _____

(List residence addresses for the past three years on the back.)

City _____ County _____ Zip _____

Phone _____

I have read the entire text of this application, and the statements therein are correct and true. (Making false statements on this application is a misdemeanor.)

_____

(Signature of Applicant)

Character references.

_____

    Name:    Address

_____

    Name:    Address

Approved ____ Disapproved _____ by _____

Competence with handgun demonstrated by _____
(to be filled in by sheriff)

Date _____ Fee Paid _____

License No. _____

---

(5)(a) Fees for concealed handgun licenses are:

(A) $15 to the Department of State Police for conducting the fingerprint check of the applicant.

(B) $50 to the sheriff for the issuance or renewal of a concealed handgun license.

(C) $15 to the sheriff for the duplication of a license because of loss or change of address.

(b) The sheriff may enter into an agreement with the Department of Transportation to produce the concealed handgun license.

(6) No civil or criminal liability shall attach to the sheriff or any authorized representative engaged in the receipt and review of, or an investigation connected with, any application for, or in the issuance, denial or revocation of, any license under ORS 166.291 to 166.295 as a result of the lawful performance of duties under those sections.

(7) Immediately upon acceptance of an application for a concealed handgun license, the sheriff shall enter the applicant's name into the Law Enforcement Data System indicating that the person is an applicant for a concealed handgun license or is a license holder.

(8) The county sheriff may waive the residency requirement in subsection (1)(c) of this section for a resident of a contiguous state who has a compelling business interest or other legitimate demonstrated need.

(9) For purposes of subsection (1)(c) of this section, a person is a resident of a county if the person:

(a) Has a current Oregon driver license issued to the person showing a residence address in the county;

(b) Is registered to vote in the county and has a voter notification card issued to the person under ORS 247.181 showing a residence address in the county;

(c) Has documentation showing that the person currently leases or owns real property in the county; or

(d) Has documentation showing that the person filed an Oregon tax return for the most recent tax year showing a residence address in the county.

(10) As used in this section, "drug diversion program" means a program in which a defendant charged with a marijuana possession offense completes a program under court supervision and in which the marijuana possession offense is dismissed upon successful completion of the diversion program. [1989 c.839 §8 (166.291 to 166.293 enacted in lieu of 166.290); 1991 c.67 §38; 1993 c.732 §2; 1993 c.735 §4; 1995 c.729 §6; 1999 c.1052 §6; 2001 c.104 §56; 2003 c.166 §1; 2005 c.22 §115; 2007 c.368 §2; 2009 c.595 §113; 2009 c.826 §§7,10; 2011 c.547 §§33,34; 2013 c.243 §§4,5; 2013 c.360 §§8,9; 2013 c.591 §§6,7; 2014 c.62 §§1,2; 2015 c.50 §§15,16; 2015 c.201 §5]

**166.292 Procedure for issuing; form of license; duration.** (1) If the application for the license is approved, the sheriff shall issue and mail or otherwise deliver to the applicant at the address shown on the application, within 45 days of the application, a wallet sized license bearing the photograph of the licensee. The license must be signed by the licensee and carried whenever the licensee carries a concealed handgun.

(2) Failure of a person who carries a concealed handgun also to carry a concealed handgun license is prima facie evidence that the person does not have such a license.

(3) Licenses for concealed handguns shall be uniform throughout the state in substantially the following form:

---

OREGON CONCEALED HANDGUN LICENSE

County_____ License Number_____

Expires_____ Date of birth_____

Height_____ Weight_____

Name_____ Address_____

Licensee's City_____ Zip_____ Photograph_____

Signature_____

Issued by_____

Date of issue_____

---

(4) An Oregon concealed handgun license issued under ORS 166.291 and this section, unless revoked under ORS 166.293, is valid for a period of four years from the date on which it is issued.

(5) The sheriff shall keep a record of each license issued under ORS 166.291 and this section, or renewed pursuant to ORS 166.295.

(6) When a sheriff issues a concealed handgun license under this section, the sheriff shall provide the licensee with a list of those places where carrying concealed handguns is prohibited or restricted by state or federal law. [1989 c.839 §9 (166.291 to 166.293 enacted in lieu of 166.290); 1993 c.625 §5; 1993 c.693 §2; 1993 c.735 §5]

**166.293 Denial or revocation of license; review.** (1) If the application for the concealed handgun license is denied, the sheriff shall set forth in writing the reasons for the denial. The denial shall be sent to the applicant by certified mail, restricted delivery, within 45 days after the application was made. If no decision is issued within 45 days, the person may seek review under the procedures in subsection (5) of this section.

(2) Notwithstanding ORS 166.291 (1), and subject to review as provided in subsection (5) of this section, a sheriff may deny a concealed handgun license if the sheriff has reasonable grounds to believe that the applicant has been or is reasonably likely to be a danger to self or others, or to the community at large, as a result of the applicant's mental or psychological state or as demonstrated by the applicant's past pattern of behavior involving unlawful violence or threats of unlawful violence.

(3)(a) Any act or condition that would prevent the issuance of a concealed handgun license is cause for revoking a concealed handgun license.

(b) A sheriff may revoke a concealed handgun license by serving upon the licensee a notice of revocation. The notice must contain the grounds for the revocation and must be served either personally or by certified mail, restricted delivery. The notice and return of service shall be included in the file of the licensee. The revocation is effective upon the licensee's receipt of the notice.

(4) Any peace officer or corrections officer may seize a concealed handgun license and return it to the issuing sheriff if the license is held by a person who has been arrested or cited for a crime that can or would otherwise disqualify the person from being issued a concealed handgun license. The issuing sheriff shall hold the license for 30 days. If the person is not charged with a crime within the 30 days, the sheriff shall return the license unless the sheriff revokes the license as provided in subsection (3) of this section.

(5) A person denied a concealed handgun license or whose license is revoked or not renewed under ORS 166.291 to 166.295 may petition the circuit court in the petitioner's county of residence

to review the denial, nonrenewal or revocation. The petition must be filed within 30 days after the receipt of the notice of denial or revocation.

(6) The judgment affirming or overturning the sheriff's decision shall be based on whether the petitioner meets the criteria that are used for issuance of a concealed handgun license and, if the petitioner was denied a concealed handgun license, whether the sheriff has reasonable grounds for denial under subsection (2) of this section. Whenever the petitioner has been previously sentenced for a crime under ORS 161.610 or for a crime of violence for which the person could have received a sentence of more than 10 years, the court shall grant relief only if the court finds that relief should be granted in the interest of justice.

(7) Notwithstanding the provisions of ORS 9.320, a party that is not a natural person, the state or any city, county, district or other political subdivision or public corporation in this state, without appearance by attorney, may appear as a party to an action under this section.

(8) Petitions filed under this section shall be heard and disposed of within 15 judicial days of filing or as soon as practicable thereafter.

(9) Filing fees for actions shall be as for any civil action filed in the court. If the petitioner prevails, the amount of the filing fee shall be paid by the respondent to the petitioner and may be incorporated into the court order.

(10) Initial appeals of petitions shall be heard de novo.

(11) Any party to a judgment under this section may appeal to the Court of Appeals in the same manner as for any other civil action.

(12) If the governmental entity files an appeal under this section and does not prevail, it shall be ordered to pay the attorney fees for the prevailing party. [1989 c.839 §9a (166.291 to 166.293 enacted in lieu of 166.290); 1993 c.735 §6; 1995 c.518 §3; 1995 c.658 §89; 1999 c.1052 §7; 2003 c.14 §65; 2007 c.202 §1; 2007 c.368 §3; 2015 c.7 §8]

**166.295 Renewal of license.** (1)(a) A concealed handgun license is renewable by repeating the procedures set out in ORS 166.291 and 166.292, except for the requirement to submit fingerprints and provide character references. A licensee may submit the application for renewal by mail if the licensee:

(A) Is an active member of the Armed Forces of the United States, the National Guard of the United States or the Oregon National Guard; and

(B) Submits with the application proof of the licensee's military orders and a copy of the licensee's military identification.

(b) An otherwise expired concealed handgun license continues to be valid for up to 45 days after the licensee applies for renewal if:

(A) The licensee applies for renewal before the original license expires;

(B) The licensee has proof of the application for renewal; and

(C) The application for renewal has not been denied.

(2) If a licensee changes residence, the licensee shall report the change of address and the sheriff shall issue a new license as a duplication for a change of address. The license shall expire upon the same date as would the original. [1989 c.839 §10; 1993 c.735 §7; 2007 c.368 §4]

**166.297 Annual report regarding revocation of licenses.** (1) The sheriff of a county shall submit annually to the Department of State Police a report containing the number of concealed handgun licenses revoked during the reporting period and the reasons for the revocations.

(2) The Department of State Police shall compile the reports submitted under subsection (1) of this section and shall submit the compilation to the Legislative Assembly biennially. [1993 c.735 §13]

**166.300 Killing or injuring another with firearm as cause for loss of right to bear arms.** (1) Any person who has committed, with firearms of any kind or description, murder in any degree, or manslaughter, either voluntary or involuntary, or who in a careless or reckless manner, kills or injures another with firearms, and who, at any time after committing murder or manslaughter or after said careless or reckless killing or injury of another, carries or bears firearms of any kind or description within this state, commits a Class A misdemeanor.

(2) Subsection (1) of this section does not deprive the people of this state of the right to bear arms for the defense of themselves and the state, and does not apply to any peace officer in the discharge of official duties or to a member of any regularly constituted military organization while on duty with such military organization. [Amended by 2011 c.597 §163]

**166.310 [Repealed by 1985 c.709 §4]**

**166.320 Setting springgun or setgun.** (1) Any person who places or sets any loaded springgun, setgun, or any gun, firearm or other device of any kind designed for containing or firing explosives, in any place where it may be fired, exploded or discharged by the contact of any person or animal with any string, wire, rod, stick, spring or other contrivance affixed to or connected with it, or with its trigger, commits a Class B misdemeanor.

(2) Subsection (1) of this section does not apply to any loaded springgun, setgun, firearm or other device placed for the purpose of destroying gophers, moles or other burrowing rodents, and does not prevent the use of a coyote getter by employees of county, state or federal governments engaged in cooperative predatory animal control work. [Amended by 2011 c.597 §164]

**166.330 Use of firearms with other than incombustible gun wadding.** Any person who uses in any firearms discharged on lands within this state, not owned by the person, anything other than incombustible gun wadding, commits a Class C misdemeanor. [Amended by 2011 c.597 §165]

**166.340** [1965 c.20 §§2,3; 1969 c.351 §1; repealed by 1981 c.41 §3]

**166.350 Unlawful possession of armor piercing ammunition.** (1) A person commits the crime of unlawful possession of armor piercing ammunition if the person:

(a) Makes, sells, buys or possesses any handgun ammunition the bullet or projectile of which is coated with Teflon or any chemical compound with properties similar to Teflon and which is intended to penetrate soft body armor, such person having the intent that the ammunition be used in the commission of a felony; or

(b) Carries any ammunition described in paragraph (a) of this subsection while committing any felony during which the person or any accomplice of the person is armed with a firearm.

(2) As used in this section, "handgun ammunition" means ammunition principally for use in pistols or revolvers notwithstanding that the ammunition can be used in some rifles.

(3) Unlawful possession of armor piercing ammunition is a Class A misdemeanor. [1985 c.755 §2; 1987 c.158 §29]

## POSSESSION OF WEAPON OR DESTRUCTIVE DEVICE IN PUBLIC BUILDING OR COURT FACILITY

**166.360** Definitions for ORS 166.360 to 166.380. As used in ORS 166.360 to 166.380, unless the context requires otherwise:

(1) "Capitol building" means the Capitol, the State Office Building, the State Library Building, the Labor and Industries Building, the State Transportation Building, the Agriculture Building or the Public Service Building and includes any new buildings which may be constructed on the same grounds as an addition to the group of buildings listed in this subsection.

(2) "Court facility" means a courthouse or that portion of any other building occupied by a circuit court, the Court of Appeals, the Supreme Court or the Oregon Tax Court or occupied by personnel related to the operations of those courts, or in which activities related to the operations of those courts take place.

(3) "Judge" means a judge of a circuit court, the Court of Appeals, the Supreme Court, the Oregon Tax Court, a municipal court, a probate court or a juvenile court or a justice of the peace.

(4) "Judicial district" means a circuit court district established under ORS 3.012 or a justice of the peace district established under ORS 51.020.

(5) "Juvenile court" has the meaning given that term in ORS 419A.004.

(6) "Loaded firearm" means:

(a) A breech-loading firearm in which there is an unexpended cartridge or shell in or attached to the firearm including but not limited to, in a chamber, magazine or clip which is attached to the firearm.

(b) A muzzle-loading firearm which is capped or primed and has a powder charge and ball, shot or projectile in the barrel or cylinder.

(7) "Local court facility" means the portion of a building in which a justice court, a municipal court, a probate court or a juvenile court conducts business, during the hours in which the court operates.

(8) "Probate court" has the meaning given that term in ORS 111.005.

(9) "Public building" means a hospital, a capitol building, a public or private school, as defined in ORS 339.315, a college or university, a city hall or the residence of any state official elected by the state at large, and the grounds adjacent to each such building. The term also includes that portion of any other building

occupied by an agency of the state or a municipal corporation, as defined in ORS 297.405, other than a court facility.

(10) "Weapon" means:

(a) A firearm;

(b) Any dirk, dagger, ice pick, slingshot, metal knuckles or milar insany sitrument or a knife, other than an ordinary pocketknife with a blade less than four inches in length, the use of which could inflict injury upon a person or property;

(c) Mace, tear gas, pepper mace or any similar deleterious agent as defined in ORS 163.211;

(d) An electrical stun gun or any similar instrument;

(e) A tear gas weapon as defined in ORS 163.211;

(f) A club, bat, baton, billy club, bludgeon, knobkerrie, nunchaku, nightstick, truncheon or any similar instrument, the use of which could inflict injury upon a person or property; or

(g) A dangerous or deadly weapon as those terms are defined in ORS 161.015. [1969 c.705 §1; 1977 c.769 §2; 1979 c.398 §1; 1989 c.982 §4; 1993 c.741 §2; 1999 c.577 §2; 1999 c.782 §6; 2001 c.201 §1; 2015 c.351 §1]

## 166.370 Possession of firearm or dangerous weapon in public building or court facility; exceptions; discharging firearm at school.

(1) Any person who intentionally possesses a loaded or unloaded firearm or any other instrument used as a dangerous weapon, while in or on a public building, shall upon conviction be guilty of a Class C felony.

(2)(a) Except as otherwise provided in paragraph (b) of this subsection, a person who intentionally possesses:

(A) A firearm in a court facility is guilty, upon conviction, of a Class C felony. A person who intentionally possesses a firearm in a court facility shall surrender the firearm to a law enforcement officer.

(B) A weapon, other than a firearm, in a court facility may be required to surrender the weapon to a law enforcement officer or to immediately remove it from the court facility. A person who fails to comply with this subparagraph is guilty, upon conviction, of a Class C felony.

(C) A firearm in a local court facility is guilty, upon conviction, of a Class C felony if, prior to the offense, the presiding judge of the local court facility entered an order prohibiting firearms in the area in which the court conducts business and during the hours in which the court operates.

(b) The presiding judge of a judicial district or a municipal court may enter an order permitting the possession of specified weapons in a court facility.

(c) Within a shared court facility, the presiding judge of a municipal court or justice of the peace district may not enter an order concerning the possession of weapons in the court facility that is in conflict with an order entered by the presiding judge of the circuit court.

(3) Subsection (1) of this section does not apply to:

(a) A police officer or reserve officer, as those terms are defined in ORS 181A.355.

(b) A parole and probation officer, as defined in ORS 181A.355, while the parole and probation officer is acting within the scope of employment.

(c) A federal officer, as defined in ORS 133.005, or a certified reserve officer or corrections officer, as those terms are defined in ORS 181A.355, while the federal officer, certified reserve officer or corrections officer is acting within the scope of employment.

(d) A person summoned by an officer described in paragraph (a), (b) or (c) of this subsection to assist in making an arrest or preserving the peace, while the summoned person is engaged in assisting the officer.

(e) An honorably retired law enforcement officer.

(f) An active or reserve member of the military forces of this state or the United States, when engaged in the performance of duty.

(g) A person who is licensed under ORS 166.291 and 166.292 to carry a concealed handgun.

(h) A person who is authorized by the officer or agency that controls the public building to possess a firearm or dangerous weapon in that public building.

(i) An employee of the United States Department of Agriculture, acting within the scope of employment, who possesses a firearm in the course of the lawful taking of wildlife.

(j) Possession of a firearm on school property if the firearm:

(A) Is possessed by a person who is not otherwise prohibited from possessing the firearm; and

(B) Is unloaded and locked in a motor vehicle.

(4)(a) The exceptions listed in subsection (3)(d) to (j) of this section constitute affirmative defenses to a charge of violating subsection (1) of this section.

(b) A person may not use the affirmative defense described in subsection (3)(e) of this section if the person has been convicted of an offense that would make the person ineligible to obtain a concealed handgun license under ORS 166.291 and 166.292.

(5)(a) Any person who knowingly, or with reckless disregard for the safety of another, discharges or attempts to discharge a firearm at a place that the person knows is a school shall upon conviction be guilty of a Class C felony.

(b) Paragraph (a) of this subsection does not apply to the discharge of a firearm:

(A) As part of a program approved by a school in the school by an individual who is participating in the program;

(B) By a law enforcement officer acting in the officer's official capacity; or

(C) By an employee of the United States Department of Agriculture, acting within the scope of employment, in the course of the lawful taking of wildlife.

(6) Any weapon carried in violation of this section is subject to the forfeiture provisions of ORS 166.279.

(7) Notwithstanding the fact that a person's conduct in a single criminal episode constitutes a violation of both subsections (1) and (5) of this section, the district attorney may charge the person with only one of the offenses.

(8) As used in this section, "dangerous weapon" means a dangerous weapon as that term is defined in ORS 161.015. [1969 c.705 §§2,4; 1977 c.207 §2; 1979 c.398 §2; 1989 c.839 §22; 1989 c.982 §5; 1991 c.67 §39; 1993 c.625 §1; 1999 c.782 §7; 1999 c.1040 §4; 2001 c.666 §§24,36; 2003 c.614 §6; 2009 c.556 §6; 2015 c.351 §2; 2015 c.709 §4]

**166.372** [1993 c.625 §3; repealed by 1996 c.16 §5]

**166.373 Possession of weapon in court facility by peace officer or federal officer.** (1) Notwithstanding ORS 166.370 (2) and except as provided in subsection (2) of this section, a peace officer, as defined in ORS 161.015, or a federal officer, as defined in ORS 133.005, may possess a weapon in a court facility if the officer:

(a) Is acting in an official capacity and is officially on duty;

(b) Is carrying a weapon that the employing agency of the officer has authorized the officer to carry; and

(c) Is in compliance with any security procedures established under subsections (3) and (4) of this section.

(2) A judge may prohibit a peace officer or a federal officer from possessing a weapon in a courtroom. A notice of the prohibition of the possession of a weapon by an officer in a courtroom must be posted outside the entrance to the courtroom.

(3) A presiding judge of a judicial district or a municipal court or the Chief Justice of the Supreme Court may establish procedures regulating the possession of a weapon in a court facility by a peace officer or a federal officer subject to the following:

(a) The procedures for a circuit court must be established through a plan for court security improvement, emergency preparedness and business continuity under ORS 1.177 or 1.180;

(b) The procedures for a justice court or a municipal court may only prohibit the possession of weapons within the area in which the court conducts business and during the hours in which the court operates;

(c) Within a shared court facility, the presiding judge of a municipal court or justice of the peace district may not establish procedures in conflict with the procedures established by the presiding judge of the circuit court; and

(d) Notice of the procedures must be posted at the entrance to the court facility, or at an entrance for peace officers or federal officers if the entrance is separate from the entrance to the court facility, and at a security checkpoint in the court facility.

(4) A judge may establish procedures regulating the possession of a weapon in a courtroom by a peace officer or a federal officer. A notice of the procedures regulating the possession of a weapon by an officer must be posted outside the entrance to the courtroom. [2001 c.201 §3; 2005 c.804 §7; 2015 c.351 §3]

**166.375 Possession of handgun or ammunition by Department of Corrections authorized staff member; rules.** (1) Notwithstanding ORS 162.135 and 162.185 or any Department of Corrections regulation, rule, policy or provision of an employment contract to the contrary, if the department has not provided a secure and locked location for the storage of personal handguns and ammunition by authorized staff, authorized staff may possess a personal handgun and ammunition in the authorized staff member's personal vehicle when the vehicle is parked in a department parking lot if the authorized staff member:

(a) Is present at a public building owned or occupied by the department;

(b) Has a valid concealed handgun license issued pursuant to ORS 166.291 and 166.292; and

(c) Has secured the personal handgun and ammunition in a closed and locked container designed for the storage of firearms inside the vehicle.

(2)(a) Authorized staff may possess and store only the amount and types of ammunition authorized by the department by written policy or rule.

(b) The department shall adopt written policies or rules to carry out the purposes of this section. The policies or rules shall include, at a minimum, procedures for and responsibilities of authorized staff when possessing and storing personal handguns and ammunition on property owned or occupied by the department under this section.

(3) As used in this section and ORS 423.045:

(a) "Authorized staff" means employees of the department and employees of the State Board of Parole and Post-Prison Supervision and Oregon Corrections Enterprises who are assigned to work in or at a public building owned or occupied by the department.

(b) "Handgun" has the meaning given that term in ORS 166.210.

(c) "Vehicle" means a vehicle that is self-propelled and that is commonly known as a passenger car, van, truck or motorcycle. [2014 c.88 §2; 2015 c.246 §1]

**166.380 Examination of firearm by peace officer; presentation of concealed handgun license.** (1) Except as provided in subsection (2) of this section, a peace officer may examine a firearm possessed by anyone on the person while in or on a public building to determine whether the firearm is a loaded firearm.

(2) A person who is licensed under ORS 166.291 and 166.292 to carry a concealed handgun may present a valid concealed handgun license to the peace officer instead of providing the firearm to the peace officer for examination. [1969 c.705 §3; 2015 c.605 §1]

**166.382 Possession of destructive device prohibited; exceptions.** (1) A person commits the crime of unlawful possession of a destructive device if the person possesses:

(a) Any of the following devices with an explosive, incendiary or poison gas component:

(A) Bomb;

(B) Grenade;

(C) Rocket having a propellant charge of more than four ounces;

(D) Missile having an explosive or incendiary charge of more than one-quarter ounce; or

(E) Mine; or

(b) Any combination of parts either designed or intended for use in converting any device into any destructive device described in paragraph (a) of this subsection and from which a destructive device may be readily assembled.

(2) As used in this section:

(a) "Destructive device" does not include any device which is designed primarily or redesigned primarily for use as a signaling, pyrotechnic, line throwing, safety or similar device.

(b) "Possess" has the meaning given that term in ORS 161.015.

(3) This section does not apply to:

(a) Persons who possess explosives as provided in ORS 480.200 to 480.290.

(b) The possession of an explosive by a member of the Armed Forces of the United States while on active duty and engaged in the performance of official duties or by a member of a regularly organized fire or police department of a public agency while engaged in the performance of official duties.

(c) The possession of an explosive in the course of transportation by way of railroad, water, highway or air while under the jurisdiction of, or in conformity with, regulations adopted by the United States Department of Transportation.

(d) The possession, sale, transfer or manufacture of an explosive by a person acting in accordance with the provisions of any applicable federal law or regulation that provides substantially the same requirements as the comparable provisions of ORS 480.200 to 480.290.

(4) Possession of a destructive device is a Class C felony. [1989 c.982 § 1]

**166.384 Unlawful manufacture of destructive device.** (1) A person commits the crime of unlawful manufacture of a destructive device if the person assembles, produces or otherwise manufactures:

(a) A destructive device, as defined in ORS 166.382; or

(b) A pyrotechnic device containing two or more grains of pyrotechnic charge in violation of chapter 10, Title 18 of the United States Code.

(2) Unlawful manufacture of a destructive device is a Class C felony. [1989 c.982 §2]

**166.385 Possession of hoax destructive device.** (1) A person commits the crime of possession of a hoax destructive device if the person knowingly places another person in fear of serious physical injury by:

(a) Possessing, manufacturing, selling, delivering, placing or causing to be placed a hoax destructive device; or

(b) Sending a hoax destructive device to another person.

(2) Possession of a hoax destructive device is a Class A misdemeanor.

(3) Notwithstanding subsection (2) of this section, possession of a hoax destructive device is a Class C felony if a person possesses, or threatens to use, a hoax destructive device while the person is committing or attempting to commit a felony.

(4) As used in this section, "hoax destructive device" means an object that reasonably appears, under the circumstances:

(a) To be a destructive device, as described in ORS 166.382 (1)(a), or an explosive, as defined in ORS 166.660, but is an inoperative imitation of a destructive device or explosive; or

(b) To contain a destructive device, as described in ORS 166.382 (1)(a), or an explosive, as defined in ORS 166.660. [1997 c.749 §1]

## SALE OR TRANSFER OF FIREARMS

**166.410 Manufacture, importation or sale of firearms.** Any person who manufactures or causes to be manufactured within this state, or who imports into this state, or offers, exposes for sale, or sells or transfers a handgun, short-barreled rifle, short-barreled shotgun, firearms silencer or machine gun, otherwise than in accordance with ORS 166.250, 166.260, 166.270, 166.291, 166.292, 166.425, 166.450, 166.460 and 166.470, is guilty of a Class B felony. [Amended by 1979 c.779 §5; 1987 c.320 §89; 1989 c.839 §23; 1995 c.729 §7; 2001 c.666 §§34,46; 2003 c.14 §§66,67; 2003 c.614 §9]

**166.412 Definitions; firearms transaction record; criminal history record check; liability; rules.** (1) As used in this section:

(a) "Antique firearm" has the meaning given that term in 18 U.S.C. 921;

(b) "Department" means the Department of State Police;

(c) "Firearm" has the meaning given that term in ORS 166.210, except that it does not include an antique firearm;

(d) "Firearms transaction record" means the firearms transaction record required by 18 U.S.C. 921 to 929;

(e) "Firearms transaction thumbprint form" means a form provided by the department under subsection (11) of this section;

(f) "Gun dealer" means a person engaged in the business, as defined in 18 U.S.C. 921, of selling, leasing or otherwise transferring a firearm, whether the person is a retail dealer, pawnbroker or otherwise;

(g) "Handgun" has the meaning given that term in ORS 166.210; and

(h) "Purchaser" means a person who buys, leases or otherwise receives a firearm from a gun dealer.

(2) Except as provided in subsections (3)(c) and (12) of this section, a gun dealer shall comply with the following before a handgun is delivered to a purchaser:

(a) The purchaser shall present to the dealer current identification meeting the requirements of subsection (4) of this section.

(b) The gun dealer shall complete the firearms transaction record and obtain the signature of the purchaser on the record.

(c) The gun dealer shall obtain the thumbprints of the purchaser on the firearms transaction thumbprint form and attach the form to the gun dealer's copy of the firearms transaction record to be filed with that copy.

(d) The gun dealer shall request by telephone that the department conduct a criminal history record check on the purchaser and shall provide the following information to the department:

(A) The federal firearms license number of the gun dealer;

(B) The business name of the gun dealer;

(C) The place of transfer;

(D) The name of the person making the transfer;

(E) The make, model, caliber and manufacturer's number of the handgun being transferred;

(F) The name and date of birth of the purchaser;

(G) The Social Security number of the purchaser if the purchaser voluntarily provides this number to the gun dealer; and

(H) The type, issuer and identification number of the identification presented by the purchaser.

(e) The gun dealer shall receive a unique approval number for the transfer from the department and record the approval number on the firearms transaction record and on the firearms transaction thumbprint form.

(f) The gun dealer may destroy the firearms transaction thumbprint form five years after the completion of the firearms transaction thumbprint form.

(3)(a) Upon receipt of a request of the gun dealer for a criminal history record check, the department shall immediately, during the gun dealer's telephone call or by return call:

(A) Determine, from criminal records and other information available to it, whether the purchaser is disqualified under ORS 166.470 from completing the purchase; and

(B) Notify the dealer when a purchaser is disqualified from completing the transfer or provide the dealer with a unique approval number indicating that the purchaser is qualified to complete the transfer.

(b) If the department is unable to determine if the purchaser is qualified or disqualified from completing the transfer within 30 minutes, the department shall notify the dealer and provide the dealer with an estimate of the time when the department will provide the requested information.

(c) If the department fails to provide a unique approval number to a gun dealer or to notify the gun dealer that the purchaser is disqualified under paragraph (a) of this subsection before the close of the gun dealer's next business day following the request by the dealer for a criminal history record check, the dealer may deliver the handgun to the purchaser.

(4)(a) Identification required of the purchaser under subsection (2) of this section shall include one piece of current identification bearing a photograph and the date of birth of the purchaser that:

(A) Is issued under the authority of the United States Government, a state, a political subdivision of a state, a foreign government, a political subdivision of a foreign government, an international governmental organization or an international quasi-governmental organization; and

(B) Is intended to be used for identification of an individual or is commonly accepted for the purpose of identification of an individual.

(b) If the identification presented by the purchaser under paragraph (a) of this subsection does not include the current address of the purchaser, the purchaser shall present a second piece of current identification that contains the current address of the purchaser. The Superintendent of State Police may specify by rule the type of identification that may be presented under this paragraph.

(c) The department may require that the dealer verify the identification of the purchaser if that identity is in question by sending the thumbprints of the purchaser to the department.

(5) The department shall establish a telephone number that shall be operational seven days a week between the hours of 8 a.m. and 10 p.m. for the purpose of responding to inquiries from dealers for a criminal history record check under this section.

(6) No public employee, official or agency shall be held criminally or civilly liable for performing the investigations required by this section provided the employee, official or agency acts in good faith and without malice.

(7)(a) The department may retain a record of the information obtained during a request for a criminal history record check for no more than five years.

(b) The record of the information obtained during a request for a criminal history record check by a gun dealer is exempt from disclosure under public records law.

(c) If the department determines that a purchaser is prohibited from possessing a firearm under ORS 166.250 (1) (c), as soon as practicable, the department may report the attempted transfer and the purchaser's name to the appropriate law enforcement agency.

(8) A law enforcement agency may inspect the records of a gun dealer relating to transfers of handguns with the consent of a gun dealer in the course of a reasonable inquiry during a criminal investigation or under the authority of a properly authorized subpoena or search warrant.

(9) When a handgun is delivered, it shall be unloaded.

(10) In accordance with applicable provisions of ORS chapter 183, the Superintendent of State Police may adopt rules necessary for:

(a) The design of the firearms transaction thumbprint form;

(b) The maintenance of a procedure to correct errors in the criminal records of the department;

(c) The provision of a security system to identify dealers who request a criminal history record check under subsection (2) of this section; and

(d) The creation and maintenance of a database of the business hours of gun dealers.

(11) The department shall publish the firearms transaction thumbprint form and shall furnish the form to gun dealers on application at cost.

(12) This section does not apply to transactions between persons licensed as dealers under 18 U.S.C. 923.

(13)(a) If requested by a transferor who is not a gun dealer, a gun dealer may request a criminal background check pursuant to ORS 166.435 or 166.438 and may charge a reasonable fee for providing the service.

(b) A gun dealer that requests a criminal background check under this subsection is immune from civil liability for any use of the firearm by the recipient or transferee, provided that the gun dealer requests the criminal background check as described in this section. [1995 c.729 § 1; 2001 c.900 §25; 2009 c.595 §114; 2009 c.826 §17; 2015 c.50 §4]

**Note:** 166.412 to 166.421 were enacted into law by the Legislative Assembly but were not added to or made a part of ORS chapter 166 or any series therein by legislative action. See Preface to Oregon Revised Statutes for further explanation.

**166.414 Fees for conducting criminal history record checks.** (1) The Department of State Police may adopt a fee schedule for criminal history record checks required under ORS 166.412 and collect a fee for each criminal history record check requested. The fee schedule shall be calculated to recover the cost of performing criminal history record checks required under ORS 166.412, but may not exceed $10 per record check.

(2) Fees collected under this section shall be paid into the State Treasury and deposited in the General Fund to the credit of the State Police Account. [1995 c.729 §2]

**Note:** See note under 166.412.

**166.416 Providing false information in connection with a transfer of a firearm.** (1) A person commits the crime of providing false information in connection with a transfer of a firearm if the person knowingly provides a false name or false information or presents false identification in connection with a purchase or transfer of a firearm.

(2) Providing false information in connection with a transfer of a firearm is a Class A misdemeanor. [1995 c.729 §3; 2001 c.1 §9]

**Note:** See note under 166.412.

**166.418 Improperly transferring a firearm.** (1) A person commits the crime of improperly transferring a firearm if the person is a gun dealer as defined in ORS 166.412 and sells, leases or otherwise transfers a firearm and intentionally violates ORS 166.412 or 166.434.

(2) Improperly transferring a firearm is a Class A misdemeanor. [1995 c.729 §4; 2001 c.1 §10]

**Note:** See note under 166.412.

**166.420** [Amended by 1989 c.839 §2; 1993 c.4 §1; 1993 c.594 §4; 1993 c.693 §1; repealed by 1995 c.729 §13]

**166.421 Stolen firearms; determination; telephone requests.** The Department of State Police may respond to a telephone request from any person requesting that the department determine if department records show that a firearm is stolen. No public employee, official or agency shall be held criminally or civilly liable for performing the investigation allowed by this section provided that the employee, official or agency acts in good faith and without malice. [1995 c.729 §5]

**Note:** See note under 166.412.

**166.422 Enforcement of ORS 166.412.** Where appropriate, a person may enforce the legal duties imposed by ORS 166.412 (7)(a) or (b), by the provisions of ORS 30.260 to 30.300 and ORS chapter 183. [1989 c.839 §12; 1995 c.729 §8; 2015 c.50 §5]

**Note:** 166.422 was enacted into law by the Legislative Assembly but was not added to or made a part of ORS chapter 166 or any series therein by legislative action. See Preface to Oregon Revised Statutes for further explanation.

**166.425 Unlawfully purchasing a firearm.** (1) A person commits the crime of unlawfully purchasing a firearm if the person, knowing that the person is prohibited by state law from owning or possessing the firearm or having the firearm under the person's custody or control, purchases or attempts to purchase the firearm.

(2) Unlawfully purchasing a firearm is a Class A misdemeanor. [1989 c.839 §15; 2011 c.662 §5]

**166.427 Register of transfers of used firearms.** (1) Whenever a person engaged in the business, as defined in 18 U.S.C. 921, of selling, leasing or otherwise transferring a firearm, whether the person is a retail dealer, pawnbroker or otherwise, buys or accepts in trade, a used firearm, the person shall enter in a register the time, date and place of purchase or trade, the name of the person selling or trading the firearm, the number of the identification documentation presented by the person and the make, model and manufacturer's number of the firearm. The register shall be obtained from and furnished by the Department of State Police to the dealer on application at cost.

(2) The duplicate sheet of the register shall, on the day of purchase or trade, be hand delivered or mailed to the local law enforcement authority.

(3) Violation of this section by any person engaged in the business of selling, leasing or otherwise transferring a firearm is a Class C misdemeanor. [1989 c.839 §16; 1993 c.4 §3; 2001 c.539 §12]

**166.429 Firearms used in felony.** Any person who, with intent to commit a felony or who knows or reasonably should know that a felony will be committed with the firearm, ships, transports, receives, sells or otherwise furnishes any firearm in the furtherance of the felony is guilty of a Class B felony. [1989 c.839 §17]

**166.430** [Amended by 1971 c.464 §1; repealed by 1989 c.839 §39]

**166.432 Definitions for ORS 166.412 and 166.433 to 166.441.** (1) As used in ORS 166.412, 166.433, 166.434, 166.435, 166.436 and 166.438, "criminal background check" or "criminal history record check" means determining the eligibility of a person to purchase or possess a firearm by reviewing state and federal databases including, but not limited to, the:

(a) Oregon computerized criminal history system;

(b) Oregon mental health data system;

(c) Law Enforcement Data System;

(d) National Instant Criminal Background Check System; and

(e) Stolen guns system.

(2) As used in ORS 166.433, 166.434, 166.435, 166.436, 166.438 and 166.441:

(a) "Gun dealer" has the meaning given that term in ORS 166.412.

(b) "Gun show" means an event at which more than 25 firearms are on site and available for transfer. [2001 c.1 §3; 2015 c.50 §6]

**Note:** 166.432, 166.433 and 166.445 were made a part of 166.432 to 166.445 by law but were not added to or made a part of ORS chapter 166 or any other series therein. See Preface to Oregon Revised Statutes for further explanation.

**166.433 Findings regarding transfers of firearms.** The people of this state find that:

(1) The laws of Oregon regulating the sale of firearms contain a loophole that allows people other than gun dealers to sell firearms at gun shows without first conducting criminal background checks; and

(2) It is necessary for the safety of the people of Oregon that any person who transfers a firearm at a gun show be required to request a criminal background check before completing the transfer of the firearm. [2001 c.1 §1; 2015 c.50 §7]

**Note:** See note under 166.432.

**166.434 Application of ORS 166.412 to all firearm transfers by gun dealers; fees for criminal background checks.** (1) Notwithstanding the fact that ORS 166.412 requires a gun dealer to request a criminal history record check only when transferring a handgun, a gun dealer shall comply with the requirements of ORS 166.412 before transferring any firearm to a purchaser. The provisions of ORS 166.412 apply to the transfer of firearms other than handguns to the same extent that they apply to the transfer of handguns.

(2) In addition to the determination required by ORS 166.412 (3)(a)(A), in conducting a criminal background check or criminal history record check, the Department of State Police shall also determine whether the recipient is otherwise prohibited by state or federal law from possessing a firearm.

(3) Notwithstanding ORS 166.412 (5), the department is not required to operate the telephone number established under ORS 166.412 (5) on Thanksgiving Day or Christmas Day.

(4)(a) The department may charge a fee, not to exceed the amount authorized under ORS 166.414, for criminal background checks required under this section or ORS 166.435 or 166.436.

(b) The department shall establish a reduced fee for subsequent criminal background checks on the same recipient that are performed during the same day between the hours of 8 a.m. and 10 p.m. [2001 c.1 §5; 2015 c.50 §8]

**166.435 Firearm transfers by unlicensed persons; requirements; exceptions; penalties.** (1) As used in this section:

(a) "Transfer" means the delivery of a firearm from a transferor to a transferee, including, but not limited to, the sale, gift, loan or lease of the firearm. "Transfer" does not include the temporary provision of a firearm to a transferee if the transferor has no reason to believe the transferee is prohibited from possessing a firearm or intends to use the firearm in the commission of a crime, and the provision occurs:

(A) At a shooting range, shooting gallery or other area designed for the purpose of target shooting, for use during target practice, a firearms safety or training course or class or a similar lawful activity;

(B) For the purpose of hunting, trapping or target shooting, during the time in which the transferee is engaged in activities related to hunting, trapping or target shooting;

(C) Under circumstances in which the transferee and the firearm are in the presence of the transferor;

(D) To a transferee who is in the business of repairing firearms, for the time during which the firearm is being repaired;

(E) To a transferee who is in the business of making or repairing custom accessories for firearms, for the time during which the accessories are being made or repaired; or

(F) For the purpose of preventing imminent death or serious physical injury, and the provision lasts only as long as is necessary to prevent the death or serious physical injury.

(b) "Transferee" means a person who is not a gun dealer or licensed as a manufacturer or importer under 18 U.S.C. 923 and who intends to receive a firearm from a transferor.

(c) "Transferor" means a person who is not a gun dealer or licensed as a manufacturer or importer under 18 U.S.C. 923 and who intends to deliver a firearm to a transferee.

(2) Except as provided in ORS 166.436 and 166.438 and subsection (4) of this section, a transferor may not transfer a firearm to a transferee unless the transfer is completed through a gun dealer as described in subsection (3) of this section.

(3)(a) A transferor may transfer a firearm to a transferee only as provided in this section. Except as provided in paragraph (b) of this subsection, prior to the transfer both the transferor and the transferee must appear in person before a gun dealer, with the firearm, and request that the gun dealer perform a criminal background check on the transferee.

(b) If the transferor and the transferee reside over 40 miles from each other, the transferor may ship or deliver the firearm to a gun dealer located near the transferee or a gun dealer designated by the transferee, and the transferor need not appear before the gun dealer in person.

(c) A gun dealer who agrees to complete a transfer of a firearm under this section shall request a criminal history record check on the transferee as described in ORS 166.412 and shall comply with all requirements of federal law.

(d) If, upon completion of a criminal background check, the gun dealer:

(A) Receives a unique approval number from the Department of State Police indicating that the transferee is qualified to complete the transfer, the gun dealer shall notify the transferor, enter the firearm into the gun dealer's inventory and transfer the firearm to the transferee.

(B) Receives notification that the transferee is prohibited by state or federal law from possessing or receiving the firearm, the gun dealer shall notify the transferor and neither the transferor nor the gun dealer shall transfer the firearm to the transferee. If the transferor shipped or delivered the firearm to the gun dealer pursuant to paragraph (b) of this subsection, the gun dealer shall comply with federal law when returning the firearm to the transferor.

(e) A gun dealer may charge a reasonable fee for facilitating a firearm transfer pursuant to this section.

(4) The requirements of subsections (2) and (3) of this section do not apply to:

(a) The transfer of a firearm by or to a law enforcement agency, or by or to a law enforcement officer, private security professional or member of the Armed Forces of the United States, while that person is acting within the scope of official duties.

(b) The transfer of a firearm as part of a firearm turn-in or buyback event, in which a law enforcement agency receives or purchases firearms from members of the public.

(c) The transfer of a firearm to:

(A) A transferor's spouse or domestic partner;

(B) A transferor's parent or stepparent;

(C) A transferor's child or stepchild;

(D) A transferor's sibling;

(E) A transferor's grandparent;

(F) A transferor's grandchild;

(G) A transferor's aunt or uncle;

(H) A transferor's first cousin;

(I) A transferor's niece or nephew; or

(J) The spouse or domestic partner of a person specified in subparagraphs (B) to (I) of this paragraph.

(d) The transfer of a firearm that occurs because of the death of the firearm owner, provided that:

(A) The transfer is conducted or facilitated by a personal representative, as defined in ORS 111.005, or a trustee of a trust created in a will; and

(B) The transferee is related to the deceased firearm owner in a manner specified in paragraph (c) of this subsection.

(5)(a) A transferor who fails to comply with the requirements of this section commits a Class A misdemeanor.

(b) Notwithstanding paragraph (a) of this subsection, a transferor who fails to comply with the requirements of this section commits a Class B felony if the transferor has a previous conviction under this section at the time of the offense. [2015 c.50 §2]

**Note:** Section 1, chapter 50, Oregon Laws 2015, provides:
Sec. 1. Section 2 of this 2015 Act [166.435] and the amendments to ORS 166.250, 166.291, 166.412, 166.422, 166.432, 166.433, 166.434, 166.436, 166.438, 166.460, 166.470, 181.150, 181.740 and 426.133 by sections 3 to 19 of this 2015 Act shall be known and may be cited as the "Oregon Firearms Safety Act." [2015 c.50 §1]

**Note:** 166.435 was enacted into law by the Legislative Assembly but was not added to or made a part of ORS chapter 166 or any series therein by legislative action. See Preface to Oregon Revised Statutes for further explanation.

**166.436 Department of State Police criminal background checks for gun show firearm transfers; liability.** (1) The Department of State Police shall make the telephone number established under ORS 166.412 (5) available for requests for criminal background checks under this section from persons who are not gun dealers and who are transferring firearms at gun shows.

(2) Prior to transferring a firearm at a gun show, a transferor who is not a gun dealer may request by telephone that the department conduct a criminal background check on the recipient and shall provide the following information to the department:

(a) The name, address and telephone number of the transferor;

(b) The make, model, caliber and manufacturer's number of the firearm being transferred;

(c) The name, date of birth, race, sex and address of the recipient;

(d) The Social Security number of the recipient if the recipient voluntarily provides that number;

(e) The address of the place where the transfer is occurring; and

(f) The type, issuer and identification number of a current piece of identification bearing a recent photograph of the recipient presented by the recipient. The identification presented by the recipient must meet the requirements of ORS 166.412 (4)(a).

(3)(a) Upon receipt of a request for a criminal background check under this section, the department shall immediately, during the telephone call or by return call:

(A) Determine from criminal records and other information available to it whether the recipient is disqualified under ORS 166.470 from completing the transfer or is otherwise prohibited by state or federal law from possessing a firearm; and

(B) Notify the transferor when a recipient is disqualified from completing the transfer or provide the transferor with a unique approval number indicating that the recipient is qualified to complete the transfer. The unique approval number is a permit valid for 24 hours for the requested transfer. If the firearm is not transferred from the transferor to the recipient within 24 hours after receipt of the unique approval number, a new request must be made by the transferor.

(b) If the department is unable to determine whether the recipient is qualified for or disqualified from completing the transfer within 30 minutes of receiving the request, the department shall notify the transferor and provide the transferor with an estimate of the time when the department will provide the requested information.

(4) A public employee or public agency incurs no criminal or civil liability for performing the criminal background checks required by this section, provided the employee or agency acts in good faith and without malice.

(5)(a) The department may retain a record of the information obtained during a request for a criminal background check under this section for the period of time provided in ORS 166.412 (7).

(b) The record of the information obtained during a request for a criminal background check under this section is exempt from disclosure under public records law.

(c) If the department determines that a recipient is prohibited from possessing a firearm under ORS 166.250 (1)(c), as soon as practicable, the department may report the attempted transfer and the recipient's name to the appropriate law enforcement agency.

(6) The recipient of the firearm must be present when the transferor requests a criminal background check under this section.

(7)(a) Except as otherwise provided in paragraph (b) of this subsection, a transferor who receives notification under this section that the recipient is qualified to complete the transfer of a firearm, has the recipient fill out the form required by ORS 166.438 (1)(a) and retains the form as required by ORS 166.438 (2) is immune from civil liability for any use of the firearm from the time of the transfer unless the transferor knows, or reasonably should know, that the recipient is likely to commit an unlawful act involving the firearm.

(b) The immunity provided by paragraph (a) of this subsection does not apply:

(A) If the transferor knows, or reasonably should know, that the recipient of the firearm intends to deliver the firearm to a third person who the transferor knows, or reasonably should know, may not lawfully possess the firearm; or

(B) In any product liability civil action under ORS 30.900 to 30.920. [2001 c.1 §6; 2015 c.50 §3]

APPENDIX: OREGON'S FIREARM STATUTES

**166.438 Transfer of firearms at gun shows; penalties.** (1) A transferor who is not a gun dealer may not transfer a firearm at a gun show unless the transferor:

(a)(A) Requests a criminal background check under ORS 166.436 prior to completing the transfer;

(B) Receives a unique approval number from the Department of State Police indicating that the recipient is qualified to complete the transfer; and

(C) Has the recipient complete the form described in ORS 166.441; or

(b) Completes the transfer through a gun dealer.

(2) The transferor shall retain the completed form referred to in subsection (1) of this section for at least five years and shall make the completed form available to law enforcement agencies for the purpose of criminal investigations.

(3) A person who organizes a gun show shall post in a prominent place at the gun show a notice explaining the requirements of subsections (1) and (2) of this section. The person shall provide the form required by subsection (1) of this section to any person transferring a firearm at the gun show.

(4) Subsection (1) of this section does not apply if the transferee is licensed as a dealer under 18 U.S.C. 923.

(5)(a) Failure to comply with the requirements of subsection (1), (2) or (3) of this section is a Class A misdemeanor.

(b) Notwithstanding paragraph (a) of this subsection, failure to comply with the requirements of subsection (1), (2) or (3) of this section is a Class C felony if the person has two or more previous convictions under this section.

(6) It is an affirmative defense to a charge of violating subsection (1) or (3) of this section that the person did not know, or reasonably could not know, that more than 25 firearms were at the site and available for transfer. [2001 c.1 §7; 2015 c.50 §9]

**166.440** [Repealed by 1989 c.839 §39]

**166.441 Form for transfer of firearm at gun show.** (1) The Department of State Police shall develop a form to be completed by a person seeking to obtain a firearm at a gun show from a transferor other than a gun dealer. The department shall consider including in the form all of the requirements for disclosure of information that are required by federal law for over-the-counter firearms transactions.

(2) The department shall make the form available to the public at no cost. [2001 c.1 §8]

**166.445 Short title.** ORS 166.432 to 166.445 and the amendments to ORS 166.416, 166.418 and 166.460 by sections 9, 10 and 11, chapter 1, Oregon Laws 2001, shall be known as the Gun Violence Prevention Act. [2001 c.1 §2]

**Note:** See note under 166.432.

**166.450** Obliteration or change of identification number on firearms. Any person who intentionally alters, removes or obliterates the identification number of any firearm for an unlawful purpose, shall be punished upon conviction by imprisonment in the custody of the Department of Corrections for not more than five years. Possession of any such firearm is presumptive evidence that the possessor has altered, removed or obliterated the identification number. [Amended by 1987 c.320 §90; 1989 c.839 §24]

**166.460 Antique firearms excepted.** (1) ORS 166.250, 166.260, 166.291 to 166.295, 166.410, 166.412, 166.425, 166.434, 166.438 and 166.450 do not apply to antique firearms.

(2) Notwithstanding the provisions of subsection (1) of this section, possession of an antique firearm by a person described in ORS 166.250 (1)(c)(B) to (D) or (G) constitutes a violation of ORS 166.250. [Amended by 1979 c.779 §6; 1989 c.839 §25; 1993 c.735 §8; 1995 c.729 §9; 2001 c.1 §11; 2001 c.666 §§35,47; 2003 c.614 §10; 2009 c.499 §5; 2015 c.50 §14]

**166.470 Limitations and conditions for sales of firearms.** (1) Unless relief has been granted under ORS 166.273 or 166.274 or 18 U.S.C. 925(c) or the expunction laws of this state or an equivalent law of another jurisdiction, a person may not intentionally sell, deliver or otherwise transfer any firearm when the transferor knows or reasonably should know that the recipient:

(a) Is under 18 years of age;

(b) Has been convicted of a felony;

(c) Has any outstanding felony warrants for arrest;

(d) Is free on any form of pretrial release for a felony;

(e) Was committed to the Oregon Health Authority under ORS 426.130;

(f) After January 1, 1990, was found to be a person with mental illness and subject to an order under ORS 426.130 that the person be prohibited from purchasing or possessing a firearm as a result of that mental illness;

(g) Has been convicted of a misdemeanor involving violence

or found guilty except for insanity under ORS 161.295 of a misdemeanor involving violence within the previous four years. As used in this paragraph, "misdemeanor involving violence" means a misdemeanor described in ORS 163.160, 163.187, 163.190, 163.195 or 166.155 (1)(b);

(h) Is presently subject to an order under ORS 426.133 prohibiting the person from purchasing or possessing a firearm; or

(i) Has been found guilty except for insanity under ORS 161.295 of a felony.

(2) A person may not sell, deliver or otherwise transfer any firearm that the person knows or reasonably should know is stolen.

(3) Subsection (1)(a) of this section does not prohibit:

(a) The parent or guardian, or another person with the consent of the parent or guardian, of a minor from transferring to the minor a firearm, other than a handgun; or

(b) The temporary transfer of any firearm to a minor for hunting, target practice or any other lawful purpose.

(4) Violation of this section is a Class A misdemeanor. [Amended by 1989 c.839 §3; 1991 c.67 §40; 1993 c.735 §11; 2001 c.828 §2; 2003 c.577 §7; 2009 c.499 §6; 2009 c.595 §115; 2009 c.826 §§8,11; 2013 c.360 §§10,11; 2015 c.50 §§17,18; 2015 c.201 §6]

**166.480 Sale or gift of explosives to children.** Any person who sells, exchanges, barters or gives to any child, under the age of 14 years, any explosive article or substance, other than an ordinary firecracker containing not more than 10 grains of gunpowder or who sells, exchanges, barters or gives to any such child, any instrument or apparatus, the chief utility of which is the fact that it is used, or is ordinarily capable of being used, as an article or device to increase the force or intensity of any explosive, or to direct or control the discharge of any such explosive, is guilty of a misdemeanor. [Amended by 1989 c.839 §26]

**166.490 Purchase of firearms in certain other states.** (1) As used in this section, unless the context requires otherwise:

(a) "Contiguous state" means California, Idaho, Nevada or Washington.

(b) "Resident" includes an individual or a corporation or other business entity that maintains a place of business in this state.

(2) A resident of this state may purchase or otherwise obtain a rifle or shotgun in a contiguous state and receive in this state or transport into this state such rifle or shotgun, unless the purchase

or transfer violates the law of this state, the state in which the purchase or transfer is made or the United States.

(3) This section does not apply to the purchase, receipt or transportation of rifles and shotguns by federally licensed firearms manufacturers, importers, dealers or collectors.

(4) This section expires and stands repealed upon the date that section 922(b) (3) of the Gun Control Act of 1968 (18 U.S.C. 922(b) (3)) and regulations pursuant thereto are repealed or rescinded. [1969 c.289 §§1,2,3,4]

**166.510** [Amended by 1957 c.290 §1; 1973 c.746 §1; 1983 c.546 §2; repealed by 1985 c.709 §4]

**166.515** [1973 c.746 §2; repealed by 1985 c.709 §4]

**166.520** [Amended by 1973 c.746 §3; repealed by 1985 c.709 §4]

**166.560** [1965 c.118 §1; repealed by 1971 c.743 §432]

**166.610** [Repealed by 1971 c.743 §432]

**166.620** [Repealed by 1963 c.94 §2]

## DISCHARGING WEAPONS

**166.630 Discharging weapon on or across highway, ocean shore recreation area or public utility facility.** (1) Except as provided in ORS 166.220, any person is guilty of a violation who discharges or attempts to discharge any blowgun, bow and arrow, crossbow, air rifle or firearm:

(a) Upon or across any highway, railroad right of way or other public road in this state, or upon or across the ocean shore within the state recreation area as defined in ORS 390.605.

(b) At any public or railroad sign or signal or an electric power, communication, petroleum or natural gas transmission or distribution facility of a public utility, telecommunications utility or railroad within range of the weapon.

(2) Any blowgun, bow and arrow, crossbow, air rifle or firearm in the possession of the person that was used in committing a violation of this section may be confiscated and forfeited to the State of Oregon. This section does not prevent:

(a) The discharge of firearms by peace officers in the performance of their duty or by military personnel within the confines of a military reservation.

(b) The discharge of firearms by an employee of the United States Department of Agriculture acting within the scope of employment in the course of the lawful taking of wildlife.

(3) The hunting license revocation provided in ORS 497.415 is in addition to and not in lieu of the penalty and forfeiture provided in subsections (1) and (2) of this section.

(4) As used in this section:

(a) "Public sign" includes all signs, signals and markings placed or erected by authority of a public body.

(b) "Public utility" has the meaning given that term in ORS 164.365 (2).

(c) "Railroad" has the meaning given that term in ORS 824.020. [Amended by 1963 c.94 §1; 1969 c.501 §2; 1969 c.511 §4; 1973 c.196 §1; 1973 c.723 §118; 1981 c.900 §1; 1987 c.447 §113; 1991 c.797 §2; 2009 c.556 §7]

**166.635 Discharging weapon or throwing objects at trains.** (1) A person shall not knowingly throw an object at, drop an object on, or discharge a bow and arrow, air rifle, rifle, gun, revolver or other firearm at a railroad train, a person on a railroad train or a commodity being transported on a railroad train. This subsection does not prevent a peace officer or a railroad employee from performing the duty of a peace officer or railroad employee.

(2) Violation of subsection (1) of this section is a misdemeanor. [1973 c.139 §4]

**166.638 Discharging weapon across airport operational surfaces.** (1) Any person who knowingly or recklessly discharges any bow and arrow, gun, air gun or other firearm upon or across any airport operational surface commits a Class A misdemeanor. Any bow and arrow, gun, air gun or other firearm in the possession of the person that was used in committing a violation of this subsection may be confiscated and forfeited to the State of Oregon, and the clear proceeds shall be deposited with the State Treasury in the Common School Fund.

(2) As used in subsection (1) of this section, "airport operational surface" means any surface of land or water developed, posted or marked so as to give an observer reasonable notice that the surface is developed for the purpose of storing, parking, taxiing or operating aircraft, or any surface of land or water when actually being used for such purpose.

(3) Subsection (1) of this section does not prohibit the discharge of firearms by peace officers in the performance of their duty or

by military personnel within the confines of a military reservation, or otherwise lawful hunting, wildlife control or other discharging of firearms done with the consent of the proprietor, manager or custodian of the airport operational surface.

(4) The hunting license revocation provided in ORS 497.415 is in addition to and not in lieu of the penalty provided in subsection (1) of this section. [1981 c.901 §2; 1987 c.858 §2]

**166.640** [Repealed by 1971 c.743 §432]

## POSSESSION OF BODY ARMOR

**166.641** Definitions for ORS 166.641 to 166.643. As used in this section and ORS 166.642 and 166.643:

(1) "Body armor" means any clothing or equipment designed in whole or in part to minimize the risk of injury from a deadly weapon.

(2) "Deadly weapon" has the meaning given that term in ORS 161.015.

(3) "Misdemeanor involving violence" has the meaning given that term in ORS 166.470. [2001 c.635 §1]

**166.642 Felon in possession of body armor.** (1) A person commits the crime of felon in possession of body armor if the person:

(a) Has been convicted of a felony or misdemeanor involving violence under the law of any state or the United States; and

(b) Knowingly is in possession or control of body armor.

(2) Felon in possession of body armor is a Class C felony.

(3) For purposes of subsection (1) of this section, a person who has been found to be within the jurisdiction of a juvenile court for having committed an act that would constitute a felony or misdemeanor involving violence has been convicted of a felony or misdemeanor involving violence.

(4) Subsection (1) of this section does not apply to:

(a) A person who is wearing body armor provided by a peace officer for the person's safety or protection while the person is being transported or accompanied by a peace officer; or

(b) A person who has been convicted of only one felony under the law of this state or any other state, or who has been convicted of only one felony under the law of the United States, which felony did not involve criminal homicide, as defined in ORS 163.005, and who has been discharged from imprisonment, parole or probation for the offense for a period of 15 years prior to the date of the alleged violation of subsection (1) of this section.

(5) It is an affirmative defense to a charge of violating subsection (1) of this section that a protective order or restraining order has been entered to the benefit of the person. The affirmative defense created by this subsection is not available if the person possesses the body armor while committing or attempting to commit a crime. [2001 c.635 §2]

**166.643 Unlawful possession of body armor.** (1) A person commits the crime of unlawful possession of body armor if the person, while committing or attempting to commit a felony or misdemeanor involving violence, knowingly:

(a) Wears body armor; and

(b) Possesses a deadly weapon.

(2) Unlawful possession of body armor is a Class B felony. [2001 c.635 §3]

### EXTREME RISK PROTECTION ORDERS

In the 2017 legislative session, Republican Senator Brian Boquist joined forces with the most liberal anti-gun legislators to pass SB 719.

SB 719 allows police officers, "family members" and "household members" to go to court and ask that another's firearms (and loosely defined "deadly weapons" ) be confiscated.

These orders are called "extreme risk protection orders." But there is no requirement to prove you are a risk, and no one is protected by them.

You do not have to have committed a crime.

You do not have to have any diagnosed mental health issues.

The order is issued solely on the word of your accuser who can claim you are a danger to yourself or others.

You are not informed that this action has been taken and only know about it when the police show up at your door demanding that you turn over your guns.

You are not accused of a crime and you are not taken into custody. If your accuser claims you are suicidal, you are not offered help. If they claim you are a danger to others you are not restrained in any way.

When the police show up you are given 24 hours to get rid of your firearms or turn them over to the police.

There is no investigation required to determine if any accusations made against you are true.

There is no due process unless you choose to go to court after your firearms have been confiscated and contest the accusations at your own expense.

Among the reasons a person may give to demonstrate that you should have your rights and property seized by the state are;
That you have ever had a DUI
You have recently used marijuana (legal in Oregon) or
If you have lawfully purchased a firearm in the last 6 months.

Boquist was the only Republican to vote for the bill.

*"Well if it can fire a lot of bullets very quickly that's a good defi.. a good place  to start ok? The let's pick it, let's say three… if you haven't hit the deer with three shots, you're a pretty lousy shot. That deer deserves to get away…. But pistols are different, you have to pull the trigger each time. An assault weapon you basically hold it, goes bdup bdup bdup.."*

— Former New York Mayor Mike Bloomberg